ANCIENT AFRICAN ANCESTRAL KNOWLEDGE

IN BLACK

ANCIENT AFRICAN ANCESTRAL KNOWLEDGE

IN BLACK

By Regina G. Ray

Also purchase at amazon.com:

Contemplations In Black
ISBN: 978-1-736935-0-9

Balance In Black
ISBN: 978-1-7365935-1-6

Kwanzaa Year Round
Annual Family Book
ISBN: 978-1-7365935-2-3

Family Fun to Learn Word Find
ISBN: 978-1-7365935-4-7

Journeying Tree of Life Journal
ISBN: 978-1-7365935-5-4

Home Reading Practice
ISBN: 978-1-7365935-6-1

Dedication
ToMy Dad

Who knew? We've had hints of former Kings and Queens in our heritage. We've had signs of high intelligence by our inventions and admirable strength and athletic ability; even in the shear Will of survival by our forefathers and mothers; but who really knew beyond a shadow of a doubt? Yes, there have been many Griots who have peeped the other side of the veil and returned to inform us of all that is there. They gave us their assurance, but how could we come to overstand the truth and reality of what their words revealed when our reality is so different?

My father dragged the family to church week after week in my youth. As a child, how could I refuse? I remember his low baritone voice that vibrated the church pew as my little hands sat upon it's rail, while Daddy belted out one of his favorite tunes "How Great Thou Art." He would even get loud at the chorus part, and he meant every word. It was an overture to the beyond; somewhere out there. Now as an adult, I've come to know that he was so right, so close to truth he could smell it. He could not see it, but he sensed its truth. He could not see it beyond his sixth grade education; as the son of a share cropper. He could not see it beyond the stresses of limitations as a Black man in America, but he knew that it was there. And indeed, as he strained to see beyond the wood carved white Jesus upon the cross that hung above the pulpit and alter, I now see that he had a sense that he was indeed singing those very words to himself, "How Great Thou Art," and he was.

In song, his spirit was alluding to himself, and his daddy, and daddy's daddy, and beyond to the beginning of time. As an adult, I have been afforded the means, education, curiosity, and time to investigate, study, and have the opportunity to peep myself the hidden mysteries that religion forbids us to seek; that school fairy tales, tall tales, and his-story confuses and obscures. What did I find? The research and awareness that I have gathered and have come to overstand has provided much assurance and knowledge of self; a privilege that my mother and father possessed, if only by faith. I can only hope that I have inherited their courage to live a life in the belief of self; enough to carry me over till truth continues to unfold and reveal itself. That rich breadth of 'our-story' still awaits its full debut to us as a people; as inheritors of a vast truth and honor of How Great We Are.

TABLE OF CONTENTS

THE GIFT

The entirety of a lifetime is all that a man or woman has; this is based upon traditional belief. We each have been presented with the *'gift of life.'* What one does with their gift is determined by many factors; some in our control, some not. Knowledge of life can increase your odds.

For those of us in America who would cut out the story of the Moors, cut out a door of return to Africa, Europe and around the world; thus confining African Americans to the slave narrative that is being enforced daily. Moors controlled the seas between the Americas and the Rock of Gibraltar to the Mediterranean Sea. Africans/Moors were established in the Americas. There was no "Discovery" by Columbus. Neither was it a misguidance that Columbus bypassed the entire land mass of North America and landed way south in the Caribbean Islands; the African descendants were already known to inhabit America. Neither, was it that he thought he was in India on the east side of the world. These false narratives were created **after the fact**, such as many other narratives of American history, to serve a specific purpose in a larger scheme of renaming Native Sons and Daughters and their lands out of their original names by the invading Northerners who sought to justify their usurp of control in the Americas.

'The Door of No Return' from where slave ships docked and dispersed in Ghana is by no means the only manner by which the Black man's worldwide presence has come to be. We have been present on every continent of the world in predominant numbers from the earliest of times. The constant enforcement of the Black American *'Slave Narrative'* is both embraced and acted upon systemically by *'white supremacy'* and internally by *'self-hate'*. It is this slave narrative that the Northern man promotes of the Black man worldwide for every culture to wrongly believe that every Black woman or man has a heritage of servitude. This narrative is actually the history of the white

man intheir feudalistic servitude, Slavic culture, and Jewish ghettos of Europe, which Northernersnow wish to project off of themselves and onto every Black woman and man globally. The Northerners carried the servitude that they had lived under in Europe to the Americas, and around the world, although under various names such as, slav, slave, peasant, indentured servant, surf, and apprentice.

The Black man, as first man; gain knowledge of the 'truth' of your story. *'Know Thyself.'* Consider 'A Kwanzaa Story':

A Kwanzaa Story
By Regina G. Ray

"In the beginning of time, the earth's lands were one. This is found in the science of Plate Tectonics. During that time there lived the first woman and man who walked the earth. As this woman and man multiplied, their dwellings spread out across the land from one end of the earth to the other end until the land began to rock, shake, and drift apart.

The gathered waters began to spill between the cracks. There was a time when one could stand with their feet straddled on two separate lands with a river running between. But soon the waters spilled so widely that man had to swim to get from one side to the other.

As waters rose, and the lands drifted further apart, each person remained on their respective lands. Eventually a boat was required to reach distant shores. This is why even today we can find this first man on every continent around the world."

Seek to learn and appreciate all cultures, because as an African descendant, you have a heritage in each. Seek to drill down beyond the lightened complexions of European conquest and colonialism, into the deep rich melanated beginnings of heroes and sheroes worldwide. Seek the *Dravidians of the Indus Valley of India*; seek out *Krishna* theBlue-Black Deity of *Hinduism;* seek out Ghengis Khan the greatest of the Samurai and the original Ninjas; search for Shaka Zulu and the Ndebele people of South Africa. Seek the true identities of the 'Hidden Ones' whose very identities were stolen such as figures of early *Greeks, Phoenicians, and Etruscans. Seek La'Lupe, Celia Cruz, Hector Lavoe,* and the *Afro* origins of *Latin* and *Hispanic* music.Learn about the *Solomonic Emperor Haile Selassie, Menelik, and Queen of Sheba of Ethiopia* and the connection of *Jamaican Rastafarians* to them. *Seek out Asar, Aset and Heru, Tutankhamen, the real Queen Nefertiti, Tehuti and Maat of Ancient Egypt* and of all the mythical figures of *pre-Egyptian times.*Learn of the preserved *Atlantian and LeMoorian* mysteries, seek out the *Moors,* the *Nubians, Cush,* and *Indus-Cush* 'mystories.' Seek the *'Hidden Ones'* who today remain, scattered in Greece, China, Nepal, Arabia, Jordan, Palestine, Hawaii, South Pacific, Indonesia, North Americans. Learn of the *Olmec* and their descendants of the*Toltec, Mayan, Incas, Aztec, and Tainos* of Central America andislands; *Seminole, Cherokee, Blackfoot, Apache,* and all Native of North America. Visit museum artifacts; dig up old maps, thrift store books, old dictionaries, encyclopedias, and oral tellings. Bring to life names of the original stories of peoples, places, bodies of water such as *the Gihon*or *River Hapi* of the Nile Valley. Recover your story and

.andmarks. Correct and expand current tellings to convert Your Story from his-story; and of your lost mysteries into a 'My-story.' Write, record, and pass on your findings so that all may know comprehensively of our cosmic beginnings and distant journeys.

In this new millennium, I encourage us to take a step back out of the boxes that we have allowed ourselves to be placed so that we can perform an examination of what is really happening. When a close examination is performed, questions arise that require corrected and appropriate answers. Here I attempt to provide a presentation of knowledge at various levels so that you may actively apply analytical thinking by using yourown capable brain cells to make a clear and conscious determination as to what best suits the purpose and objective of how you choose touse the *'gift of life.'*

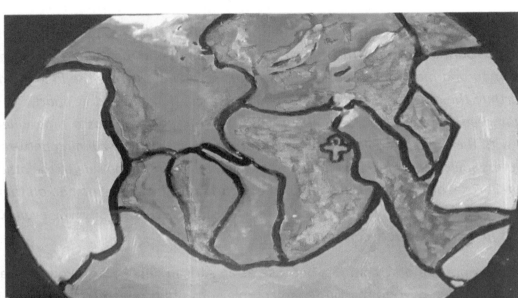

IN THE BEGINNING

The word *'beginning'* is synonymous with *'creation'* and implies *'a start'*, as in *'the firsttime.'* Yet, in the case of Earth, *'beginning'* or *'creation'* can mean *'a new start'*, as in *'out with the old, and in with the new.'* This definition conforms to the many evolutionary changes that have taken place on Earth over time. These terms are not stagnant, but instead carry a sense of fluidity, because *life is like a river.*

Time is quite long and the presence of *'man on earth'* is equivalent to a *'blink of an eye'* in regards to the age of planet Earth. There are many creatures and geographical formations that were created in past times that are no longer with us in this age; and there are some that continue. Speaking of ages, review here the devised past ages of Earth:

ERA	PERIOD	AGE	
PRECAMBRIAN	Hadean Aeon	Priscoan	4600million years ago
Archean Aeon			4000 million years ago
Proterazole Aeon			2500million years ago
PALEOZOIC	Cambrian	Invertebrates	570 million years ago
Ordovician			505 million years ago
Silurian			438 million years ago
Devonian	Fishes		408 million years ago
Carboniferous			360 million years ago
Permian	Amphibians		286 million years ago
MESOZOIC	Triassic	**(First Dinosaurs)**	245 million years ago
Jurassic			208 million years ago
Cretaceous		**(Extinction of Dinosaurs)**	144 million years ago
CENOZOIC	Tertiary	Paleocene	65.5 million years ago
Eocene			57.8 million years ago
Oligocene			36.6 million years ago
Miocene			23.7million years ago
Pliocene			5.3 million years ago
(Earliest Humans appear)	Quaternary	Pleistocene	1.6 million years ago
+Ice Age begins)	Ice Age ends	Holocene	10 thousand years ago

As you can see, Earth has existed for millions of years. The odds of Earth disappearing is improbable. However, the extinction of creatures or living thingson the earth is likely; whereas many creatures and plants have been lost to extinction over the span of time.

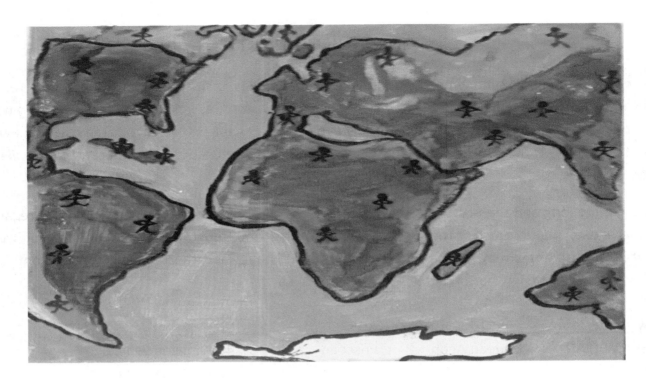

EARTH

There are many fun facts to learn about this planet on which we live. Did you know that you are an astronaut upon a big ship that spins approximately one thousand miles per hour? Many events and occurrences have taken place across the entire globe over a vast distance and over an extensive amount of time; both before humans arrived on the scene and following. The Earth has undergone many precessions; Life itself has undergone many evolutionary progressions to arrive at where we are today. You must study in order to know about as many of these events as possible. Awareness of this knowledge will assist in a proper orientation of one's place in the continuum of time. I hope you are ready for takeoff – 3 – 2 – 1 – let's go!

Scientific findings tell us that Earth is at least 4.54billion years old. Its radius is 3,950 miles (6,356 km), and the circumference around the equator is 24,901.461 miles (40,075.017 km).

> "Earthhas many motions-[1] it spins on its axis(1,037 mph),
> [2]it travels around   the Sun, and [3] it moves with the Sun through
> our Galaxy. Thesemotions accountfor the changes in the visibility
> of stars in the nightsky, and for thechanges in seasons."
> [AstronomyToday,Chaisson & McMillan]

The cosmic bodies of the sky exert gravitational pulls and pushes that maintain the distances and orientations between them in a dance of cyclic patterns. One extraordinary feature of Earth'smotion is the leaning of its polar axis. The 'polar axis' is an imaginary pole that passes through the North Pole of Earth, through Earth's center, and then out the opposite end at the South

Pole. This polar axis maintains a tilt of close to 23.5 degrees as the earth rotates and follows its path around the Sun.

> One spin = 24 hour period = 1 day
>
> One path around the Sun = 365 spins = 365 days/year

Within Earth's spin pattern there is another rotation that occurs; there is a progression as the axis forms a cone that extends from Earth's core to a distance above the planet where the top of the cone forms a 360 degree pattern (a circle). Like a spinning top, this pattern can be expressed as a 'wobble.' This wobble is called a *'Precession'* and it takes Earth 26,000 years to complete this cone pattern. *The Earth renews itself every 26,000 years through one of its four major elements of earth, wind, water, and fire.* [A.E.O.]

> It takes the Earth 26,000 years to complete a *'Precession'*

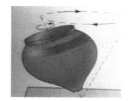

THE COSMOS

Earth is filled with a plethora of everything, including you. How did this come to be? Let's begin with the universe. Planet Earth is part of a larger rotating system called a universe. The universe is external to Earth, and includes many galaxies. Earth's galaxy is called the *Milky Way*. Earth is one of nine planets in our galaxy. The nine planets that exist in the *Milky Way* galaxy all revolve around one Sun, yet each planet has their own moon or moons. Earth is the third planet from the Sun and has only one moon. The planet Mercury is the closest planet to the Sun. Altogether, the Sun, nine planets, and moons make up the *Milky Way* galaxy.

PLANETS	COSMIC BODIES	*DISTANT STAR CONSTELLATIONS	
Mercury	Sun	Andromeda	Hercules
Venus	Moons	Aquarius	Hydra
Earth	Asteroids	Aries	Indus
Mars	Black holes	Cancer	Leo
Jupiter	Satellites	Canes	Orion
Saturn	Comets	Cassiopeia	Pegasus
Uranus	Stars	Corona	Pisces
Neptune	Galaxies	Draco	Sagittarius
Pluto	Quasars	Gemini	Ursa
(*short listing)			

The stars that are seen in the night sky are distant suns, planets, and cosmic bodies that exist farther away from Earth, or in other individual galaxies. So, as you can see, creation is quite a big deal. Can you imagine thousands, maybe millions of other galaxies like the one that we live in? Altogether, the universe and all that exist in it, is creation. Creation can be categorized as 1) on a *large scale* as the universe; 2) on a *medium scale* as our Milky Way galaxy, 3) or can be viewed on a *small scale* that refers to only Earth. View the stars on a nice clear night to see the cosmic arrangements that surround Earth.

There exists a great many religious beliefs, mythological stories, archeological findings, and scientific calculations that account for a piece of the puzzle to the mysteries of creation and how it has come to be. And then, there is You. You too are a piece of the puzzle of creation.

REALMS OF EXISTENCE

The Physical Realm
So far we've learned a few facts about planet Earth, its age, and its orientation in the universe. Earth is material matter that exists in four basic forms; *soil (earth), water, fire, and air.* These are known as the *'four basic elements'* of Earth. These basic elements together, account for the *'physical realm'* of Earth. The physical realm is made up of everything in our *environment* that we can see and touch, e.g., trees, butterflies, rain, sunshine, clothes, cars, dogs, humans, food, electronics, etc. As humans we interact with our environment by our *senses* of *touch, see, taste, hear, and smell.* There are tiny physical things also that can little be seen by the naked eye. Such physical things include the air, sound waves, light waves, microscopic bugs, dust, spores, and more. Man has made instruments to detect and measure such invisible physical elements. For example, thermometers are used to measure the temperature of air; a radio receiver may detect sound waves; and a magnifying glass or a microscope helps the eye to see smaller things such as bugs and microscopic bacteria.

The Non-Physical Realm
The non-physical realm is special. While it is invisible, we can know that it exists through our senses. Examples include feelings and emotions, instincts, thoughts, and other cognitive states of being. This realm is sometimes referred to as *'touchy-feely'* and there exists a space where the physical realm touches this non-physical realm. This touch point assists in our awareness that unseen things do exist, and helps us to gain an overstanding of how unseen things in the non-physical realm work. This non-physical realm has been the subject of various studies, sciences, and religions from the beginning of human existence. There is a body of ancient knowledge of this non-visible realm that has been handed down and maintained over many centuries.

TIME CHART

1 Minute = 60 seconds	1 Year = 12 months
1 Hour = 60 minutes	1 Decade = 10 years
1 Day = 24 hours	1 Century = 10 decades = 100 years
1 Week = 7 days	1 Millennium = 10 centuries = 1000 years
1 Month= 4 weeks	1 Epoch = 1 million years
1 Aeon = one billion years	

Both man and knowledge began in**East Africa** known as the *'Cradle of Civilization'*is actually the *'Temple of Civilization'* whereas its foundation is built from*Ascended Ancient Knowledge.*From this high point, man migrated outward across the globe. Ancient temples, pyramids, and astrological structures built by the Ancients can be found across the globe.In this way ancient knowledge has been spread worldwide and is even part of our western heritage today.This body of ancient knowledge was once thought to be a great threat to the people of northern regions of the world, who received it during the latter part of the B.C. calendar Era, starting atapproximately 300 B.C. Initially,these Northernerscould not relate to the knowledge, so in their early recordings of the knowledge, they began to change the names and places in an effort to embrace the knowledge as their own. The concepts within the ancient knowledge conflicted with their traditional practices and beliefs. As a consequence of this offense, misinterpretations, and misunderstandingsthe northern leaders and their religious authorities began to burn all of the people and documents that knew and contained the ancient knowledge. Those who valued the ancient knowledge hid away the documents that they possessed and continued their learning of them by an 'underground' method such as behind locked doors, in cellars, and in secret meetings. Thus, the ancient knowledge was hidden away from common folk in order to preserve it.

The ancient knowledge was brought to the Americasby **MoorTemple**membersand then by the secret societyof **Freemasons**from Europein their travels to NorthAmerica andSouthAmerica. Moor Rites Temples and societies were taken over by Northerners during the weakening and enslavement of the Moors in America. However, the use of this knowledge continued in the development of the new American government. It was also used in the architectural design of Washington D.C., the nation's capital city. It has come to represent all *Medical Science Communities.* The knowledge continued to arrive onto the shores of the Americas by way of the Africans who found themselves in the grips of bondage. Native traditions preserved aspects of the knowledge in their culturesuntil today.Now however, only a remnant of this knowledge remains in the minds of African, Native and Moor Americans due to capitalistic and commercial distractions.

Over time this ancient knowledge continues to emerge and has been put into use by Northerners, although, the knowledge is not a part of the western mainstream education system. As a result, there are still many who are unfamiliar with it. Today the knowledge is so extensively used that it is now *'hidden in plain sight.'*

A NEW ORIENTATION

A new orientation of perception is required in order to absorb the ancient knowledge;a total angular adjustment of mental perception, away from programmed northern thought patterns isrequired. The start of this adjustment involves learning new vocabulary, definitions, and overstandings.

In addition to a new orientation, personal disposition is a strong factor in the realization of ascended knowledge. As individuals, we each differ in strengths and weaknesses. In this way we each have a unique role that we play in this drama called life. Everything is not for everybody, and each person has a sense of their own potential and limitations. Within the infinite differences that exist across humanity, there remain a few things that we all have in common and need of. It is in these commonalities that we should become seekers of our reality, rather than what has been previously put forth by others. The knowledge has been spread to the four corners of the earth, whereas all religions stem from some aspect of Kemetic knowledge.

The papyri that were distributed to many lands is knowledgethat originated with our African forefathers and foremothers of antiquity. In order to grasp a full overstanding means you will have to comprehend your existence of more than tens of thousands of years ago. You must become a time traveler through the power of your DNA, to a time when we each shared a common melanated ancestry and heritage.

Previous European stories that have been put forth and debated widely and profusely involve the theories of *'**Evolution**'*of Darwinism, and the theory of *'Creation'* by Christians. For the African, our beginning is contained in neither. Our existence came about tens of thousands of years prior.*The Ancients* were not primitive nor were they the savages that we have been erroneously taught to believe. The *Ancients* are our *'Ascended Ancestors'* who possessed **High Knowledge** of the **Creator** and the creation. The ancient knowledge subscribesnot to any religion. Religion is a latter-day inventionby mankind. The early Kemetic Knowledge is 'truth' and factual.The presented knowledge is of the very basics of life; of how we are constructed both physically and spiritually; with spirituality being ourhighest and greatest power, yet least familiar to us. The ancient knowledge is a knowledge that exists in its highest form. There is none that is more informative to the human psyche'of its structure – that is of who, what, when, how, and why man exists and the true purpose that our presence fulfills; what started it all, and to what means and end does it lead.Once we come to learn the ancestral 'knowledge of self', we will be able to pass on to our future selves (our children) that which is required to continue a successful fulfillment of purpose.

Many hidden documents have yet to be made public. Few people have had access to the information in its entirety, yet and still its presence continues to reveal itself or be confirmed by the technological advancements of today. There exist isolated Gurus in the east who possess and share what knowledge they know of the ancients. This has been one way that the information slowly emerges and its manifestations become apparent to us. Yet, ascended teachings are little promoted because they politically violate the Christian edicts of'*Doctrine of Discovery*' and '*Inquisition*'; *both are edicts* of '*white supremacy*'.

News Item:

Today, televised documentaries dare you to acknowledge the African origins that you see painted on pyramid walls and in findings across the globe- over the white wash that it is attempting to convince you of, by completely ignoring the presence of Africans globally and by attempting to plantNortherners into the African story.

Nefertiti   Queen Ti   Akhenaten**Fake** Berlin Bust of Nefertiti

photos

According to two experts, the European style statue claimed to be *Queen Nefertiti* of Egypt is a fake that was produced in Berlin, Germany, is less than 100 years old, and is referred to as the 'Berlin Bust.' It is not made of stone as all other Egyptian statues. It is made of a soft lime stone covered in plaster, with a style unlike any artifact in Egypt, but exactly the style of statues produced in German busts; that is having the arms cut off at the shoulders. Also, the bust is unfinished and missing an eyeball; *"was made by Gerardt Marks on orders of the German archeologist Ludwig Borchardt" as reported by CBC News, May 9, 2009*. Although, this has long been identified as a fake and is a continued attempt to insert the European into the African story, the fake statue appears in every book and documentary presented on Ancient Egypt. I have of recent seen televised never before seen papyrus paintings depicting this same white female Nefertiti figure (more fakes). This and many other attempted re-writings of history via the internet is a method of *culture theft* used to gain power and control is referred to as **'Arrogance of Ignorance'**. This same method is being used in the establishment of an Israeli state. Europeans have found success in this fraudulent method around the world as they insert or take over governments, and usurp cultures and lands from Native peoples. For those who resist, they impose embargos or similar detrimental controls.

We must become seekers of the Ascended Knowledge that our Ancestors toiled tirelessly to preserve on our behalf. The knowledge is the basis of all sciences that exist today; in it we must again locate our path of purpose. Once a person gains an overstanding of how and who they are, they will be better prepared and equipped to carry out their purpose and reach their highest potential toward a powerful, positive, and productive life.

EARLY MYTHOLOGIES OF CREATION

Early mythologies tell the story of jealousy and rebellion in the heavens between the *Great Mother* and her first born son who was incomplete from birth. Faced with doubts of his incomplete existence, he became filled with a jealous spirit which he projected onto his Mother whom he held responsible for the foul birth. His jealousy consumed him as he observed the power of the *Great Mother* in all of her glory, creating. The wretched soul, deprived of proper balance, sought to make a creation of his own over which he would take rulership. He visited Earth and walked about, up and down to survey its gardens in hopes to become enlightened by his options.

He embarked upon a series of experiments involving *alternative creation practices* and *genetic blending* to develop new life. Because this soul was incomplete by its lack of feminine balance, he sought his creation to be likewise, in his image. The incomplete deity came to settle upon the idea of man alone, not as in earlier designs, but rather as man in singularity, yet as a whole. These details concur with the traditions of Greece.

> *The Greeks made their gods in their own image. That had not entered the mind of man before. Until then, gods had had no semblance of reality. In Egypt, they were unlike all living things…In Greece alone in the ancient world people were preoccupied with the visible; they were finding the satisfaction of their desires in what was actually in the world around them. The sculptor watched the athletes contending in the games and he felt that nothing he could imagine would be as beautiful as those strong young bodies. So he made his statue of Apollo.*   [Mythology, Edith Hamilton, pg.7]

> *These two stories of the creation, --the story of the Five Ages, and the story of Prometheus and Eimetheus --different as they are, agree in one point. For a long time certainly throughout the happy **Golden Age**, only men were upon the earth, there were no women. Zeus created these later, in his anger at Prometheus for caring so much for men.*   [Mythology, Edith Hamilton, pg.86]

This Greek mythology speaks of a path from where a later day creation of mankind arose. The Olympus pantheon of deities is well documented, even worship of them continues into modern ages. You will find formal ceremony on display at the start of the *Olympic Games*, during the torch lighting ceremony, at which time all hales are made to Zeus, Apollo and the remainder of the patrons of Olympia in an unbroken tradition from the very first Olympic Games of Greece.

In the mythologies of Greece, as in biblical accounts in the book of Genesis (the Genetic making of 2nd man), woman appears as an afterthought over an unspecified amount of time following the creation of men. As to what extent of truth lay within these biblical and Greek stories, another commonality that they share is a demonstration that balance cannot exist without the presence of the feminine energy.

ANCIENT KEMETAN CREATION MATTERS
The best disguise is confusion.
The easiest story to write is fiction.
The strongest is always presumed the winner.
These are the methods of how truth has come to be hidden in plain sight, while we are caught up in distractions.

Finally, we as Native Sons and Daughters can come to know our true story, in our own words.
In the beginning was the *Great Mother*. She gave birth to the first deities. Details of the beginning are of an African origin, and is representative ofhuman life. African origins predate all and any Greek mythologies. The African storybegan prior to and encompasses its Kemetic story well beyond present day timelines.

Evidence of human habitation in Egypt stretches back tens
of thousands of years. It was only in about 6000 BCE
however, that widespread settlement began in the region.

[Khan Academy.com]

The **Nile Valley** story of Kemet begins in the heart of **Central Africa** where the first cataracts are located. The Nile flows northward from its southern internal regions that includes Zaire, Uganda, Kenya, Tanzania, Sudan, Cush (modern day Ethiopia), and even connects to Lake Victoria. Early man first dwelled in these internal regions; man followed the flow of the river northward.

Pre-history is any related event prior to 4500 B.C. The African story predates, and is therefore 'SEPARATE AND APART' from the recordings ofhis-story. The first recorded Dynasty was recorded 3150 B.C. – 2686 B.C., yet, kings and pharaohs existed prior to this recorded time. The Kemetic story had started long before Europeans were able to read, write, and record history.

Hisstory, however, began as late as 800 B.C. with the arrival of Homer's*Iliad*. The *Iliad* was Europe'sfirst book. The *Iliad of Homer* is an epic tale of two rival cultures, *Sparta* and *Troy* of Greece. It contains every aspect of creative writing that a story can possess, and it set a high bar as a blueprint for all that would follow. It also gives a glimpse into the early eastern European life of the Greeks. In the Greek literature that follows however, fanciful imaginings of the grandeur of Olympia overtook Greek writings with stories of the Olympic Gods. It was quite obvious that the inspiration came directly from influences of Kemetic mythology,as Greekphilosophers frequently traveled to Egypt to learn in its schools and vast libraries, prior to Greek invasion and occupation of Egypt (Kemet).

> *Shakespeare's poem of "Venus and Adonis" which is at root mythology fleshed in a human form. Again and again the Egyptian Mythos furnishes a prototype that will suffice to account for a hundred Folk-tales….This origin of our Folk-Lore may be found a hundred times over in the "Wisdom of old Egypt."*
>
> *[Gerald Massey, Ancient Egypt – Light of the World, 1907.]*

More important than later day Greek fanciful imaginings, is the early Ascended knowledge of African Kemet in all of her deeply dark melanated hues. Direct and obvious correlations can be readily found between ourselves as African descendants in common with the images of our Kemetic Ancestors who preserved images from antiquity of and about themselves on papyrus leaf, on temple paintings, and in carvings of full statured stone that indeed to us today serve as a privilege of monumental proportionsto witness, whereas *"Nothing we learn about them is alien to ourselves."[Hamilton]*

Despite a modern day *whitewashing* of the Kemetic story by a continuous process of removing or changing African images and slowly substituting European associations, we as African descendants find in the original faces and physiques of Kemetic preservations that they are unmistakably our African brothers and sisters, whereas Egypt too resides squarely on the African continent. Given the breadth, the depth, and the earliness, of Kemetic Ancestral monumental accomplishments, it is as if the Kemetic people arrived to earth with skill and tools in hand.

> **Past Names of Africa:***Alkebulon–(used by the Moors, Nubians,Numidians, Khart-Haddans (Carthaginians), and Ethiopians.) Other past names include - Ortigia, Libya, and Ethiopia*
>
> *[Life , by Rukewve Ochuko]*
>
> *More names – Eden, Kemet, Put, Atlanta, Sudan, Cush*

Public agendas have no doubt avoided the never-taught Kemetic stories,and of the associated deeply brown skin tones in fear of inspiring young African minds to godliness. Such an inclusive lesson would have revealed that the *'the birth of the world'*and civilization came at the commencement of the dark continent; where all things were new and all spiritual inheritances have since been retained. Over time the arms of *Ancestral Africa* have stretched around each horizon step by step like an eternal embrace. African ancestral arms welcomed all its people and developing culturesthat were to come; wherever her children settled. The evidence that is present in all early cultural developments confirm African beginnings; as early as 3300 B.C. in the *Indus Valley Civilization*; to the 1500 B.C. *Olmec Civilization* in the Americas; to Indo-China as early as 4,000 B.C.,and all that has followed;prior and since.

European migrations began with the Medieval-voyages of Christopher Columbus in 1492 A.D. The European colonizing of China, India, Australia, Africa, Hawaii, Caribbean, North and South America etc. that followed, introduced the modern day expressed blending of the non-equatorial migrants into darker southern, western and eastern regions, resulting internationally in the whitening and lightening of African cultures that are seen in present day populations around the globe. And still, through all time, the Kemetic story continues to reverberate globally as its anticipated mysteries continue to unfold. Kemet inspires a comfort of assurity that the African American is **not *lost at sea*** as presumed, but in fact, is not lost at all from the path that leads from melanated beginnings in the Mother land into all lands beyond.

KEMETIC BEGINNINGS

It is from the primordial waters the first deities arose; paired polar energies.
The waters yield all at its assigned time, two by two; male & female, yin & yang,
positive& negative.

AMN / AMNT - *Hidden spark of life + its opposite*
NU / NUNUT - *Primordial unformed mass + its opposite*
KU / KUKHET- *Qualities of Light + its opposite*
HEH / HEHET - *Qualities of Infinity + its opposite*
*These first deities represent the **first key** to the mysteries of the creation of*
everything. They are amongst the most ancient symbols of shared energies of unity.
[Amenuti Narmer, Grandmother Africa.com]

The four couplings of energy, *Primordial deities*, represent the *ANKH*. The *ANKH* represents the first key to the mysteries of '*The Creation of Everything*.' The *ANKH* means more than life. It is the most ancient symbol of a code of sounds whose intonations conform to the 'Principles' and 'Order' dictated by *Maat (Order)* and *Tehuti (Vibration)*. The four deities each possess their own forces.
* At the center of the zodiac from the temple at Dendera, the Great Mother is seen carrying the feather of Maat. The Principles of Maat were ushered in by the Great Mother from the beginning of creation.
*Tehuti is the companion energy of balance to Maat. His vibration is in harmony with the subjective realm of the first Aeon where the unchanging Creator resides.

The Kemetic primal deities represent **Principles** and **Universal Laws**of the 'spiritual realm'; together**Order** accompanies creation. From the summoning of the spiritual realm, the physical realm can then manifest (exist); emerge from the primal waters. So you see, because balance exists from the beginning, creation is permitted to successfully move forward. The schematics of the build of creation can be found in the **Ennead**. (*Secrets of the Ennead: ennead means nine, e.g. nine planets, nine electrons; as above so below*).

The Early creation that followed directly from the '*Great Mother*' demonstrates a creation of *balance* between both the masculine energy and the feminine energy equally. This is the path of creation that came to be tens of thousands of years ago in Africa; the African creation that came to be in Kemet. The beginnings of Africa and Kemet reign from the stars. It too began in shared realms of spirit and flesh; of winged animal bodies with human heads, and of human bodies with animal heads, some with wings and some not. This creation by the *Great Mother* differed from the creation of her half berthed son. Because the *Great Mother* has clear consciousness of her connection to the *Great Father*, both masculine and feminine energies are contained within her essence.   The successful births of the first deities arose out of *Her* primal waters, each in complete harmony and unison. They possessed both feminine and masculine energies in equal portions, and thus,in a balanced state, came into existence.   In this useful state of balance, each deity commenced to carry out their designated purposes in creation.

Schematic Diagram of Kemetic Beginnings

UNCHANGING CREATOR 1st Aeon

THE **GREAT MOTHER**& Creation 2nd Aeon
Set
Maat – Tehuti
AMN/AMNT - NUN/NUNUT - KU/KUKHET - HEH/HEHET
Nun
Atum
Atum – Ra(life force)------------------------|
              | |
Shu(air) Tefnut(moisture)

Geb(earth)   Nut(sky)

Set_____Nephthys | Asar | Aset   Ra
          | |--------|------------|
Anubis / Kebhehut Horus /Hathor / Soshat

Within the build of creation, deities of high vibratory frequency fluxed in and out between realms in performance of their designated works for which they were created. *Intellect* reigned supreme from the heavens (the spiritual realm). A place was to be prepared in this physical realm through the *feminine energy* of *'Manifestation'*according to the*masculine intellect*of the *'Master Builder'*, worthy on which intellect would dwell, free from earthen dust. Chemistry and high science was in full swing as creation produced life forms of creatures that were conducive to the worst aspects of Earth's atmospheric activity, and equipped to traverse the most inhospitable of its terrains. The gardens of soft flora served nutritional needs.

The simpler forms of life had taken different paths in creation. The most simplistic and prolific of paths were those that the waters seeded across creation. Some creations remained in the waters, some emerged upon dry land, and some reside in betwixt. The designs of creation freely roamed the terrains of the planet.

This was a Universal Ag*e* when all of creation was in harmony with the Earth. The *Primal Waters* had just begun to disperse the potential of her immeasurable eternal energies; infinity lay within till thought or word disturbed still waters; for it is as simple as one word needed to create.

As for the creation of the new beings (Nubians) of man, and woman, our build was summoned from the beginning, complex as we are. We need only look as far as the *Stars*, to the *Ennead*, to the*Ancestors,* to the *Elders*, to our *children*, the *tips of our fingers and nose*, then back again by way of within; to our words, into our gut, to our root, up to the sacral genitals, to the heart, to ears & eyes, then to gray matter that connects again to the stars. You are first spirit, then earthen dust, then spirit to spirit. These are the places we have been given to dwell. The *Supreme Creator* tarries in the midst.

FALLEN STARS

At the beginning of the end of Egypt, there were no Hebrew captives in Egypt as is taught in biblical tales. We are they who were driven out of Egypt, but not as captives, rather as the original inhabitants, when invaders continuously took charge over the riches of Egypt's coveted culture and cities along her Nile River. Forty years of wandering in the desert translates into our four hundred years of becoming spiritually dead vessels of disobedient Kemetans, caught up in the bonds of slavery in the west (land of the dead); we are they of the prophesy, of which it had to be because it actually has occurred. The *Book of the Coming Forth By Day*, referred to as the funerary book of Egypt, details the journey of its people at the time of bodily or spiritual death. The*path of Maat*was the path of our forefathers and foremothers, before being led astray by 'Pharonic egotism,' vanity, and distraction; a deviation from the path of *Maat* that was divinely ordained from our beginning. *Concerning This Life & the Afterlife:*

> *This was the knowledge of Kemet in connecting this world to the Afterlife. Kemet was trying to find a physical way to accomplish a human battery and ultimately to the Great Mother battery. They were trying to find a way via 'fermentation' and 'embalming' to preserve the vehicle inside the physical reality as you pass into the Afterlife. To manifest back into reality, you must absorb 'Prana' from the air. Mummy cats served as the battery of 'Prana.'*
>
> *[Sevan Bomar]*

The skill craft of fermentation (alchemy)= Preserving the soul for re-animation back to life

This attempt at and artificial resurrection/reincarnation was in opposition to and a departure from what the *Creator*had ordained. For this departure from our designated path, we as a people spiritually entered the land of Nod, the Netherland, the place of the wandering dead, the west.

> *Nod is the underworld, Netherland of division. Anywhere outside of Truth is Nod. Outside of Truth, something exists. …The something is called 'shade', the shadow. Your shadow is not the real you; it is cast as a shadow of you. It is the realm of Nod, the Netherland. Whenever someone lies, they enter into Nod…There you become lost. [Sevan Bomar]*

Did I mention previously that the *Great Mother* carried with her the feather of *Maat* from the beginning? She did. So, why would an alternate path other than that summoned by the *Great Mother* be sought by man? The pyramids represent a tower, a bypass to the stars; a way to give man control and power over life and death; a justification to no longer abide by the *Laws and Principles of Maat* that had been ordained by the *Creator*, ushered in by the *Great Mother* from the beginning.

Rebellion, from the start, began in the heavens. The rebellion was against the feminine energy. This has been man's challenge from the start. It is the woman who berths and nurtures the whole of the world; from where all things emerge. Religions that oppress the feminine energy and implement patriarchal systems of control around the globe got its start at Earth's beginning with the deformed deity, Set. [https://www.youtube.com/live/OQSL913d9ag?feature=share][Ron Hayes].Perhaps Set serves the purpose of Earth's 'necessary evil.'

Earth's Drama:
Mother gives birth to incomplete Son (Set) – Son (Ego) seeks the undoing of the Mother – Son sets himself up in the sky between the Mother and the creation in order to be worshiped – Men create patriarchal religions, ignores Maat, develops his own laws and government – the world proceeds into the chaos of man's mind – Mothers and daughters suffer---The Earth suffers. The End

Characters of Earth's Drama:
The Unchanging Creator – in the first Aeon
The Great Mother – in the second Aeon
The Son –*Set, Dagan, Baal, Allah, Jesus, Yahweh, Elohim, Jehovah, Nyonkopon, Obatala, Wakan-Tonka, the Pope,* etc. depending upon your time and location.

Patriarchal Religions of Earth's Drama:
Pharonic rulers, Babylon, Judaism, Christianity, Sufism, Hindu, Islam, Zen, Chen, Zoroastrianism, Sikhism, Freemasonry, Buddhism, Taoism, Vatican, KKK, Police, Democratic & Republican Parties, Gangs, The Mob, etc.

Engagements of Patriarchal Religions& Systems:
Worship = war-ship
Suppression of women = physical violence, mental violence, spiritual ostracizing
Corruption & Theft = collection of monies, drugs, trafficking
Control& power= ego
Criminalize & Imprison– Black bodies for profit

Patriarchal suppression continues today as women seek inclusivity to the riches of the world; seek participation in political arenas; seek support by public funds medically for themselves and their children; seek equal pay, education, and respect. Women too must seek a way off the path of down which she has been led. She must follow the path of *Maat*, teach her daughters *Maat*, and become *Maat* again.

An appropriate and dignified path must again be established to lift daughtersand women off the path of poverty and dependence. It is these that expose women to the violence she encounters daily. The Earth suffers from aggressive activities and will continue to suffer as long as the feminine energy suffers—Unless, however, the original man, to whom *Maat* was delivered, lift up the staff of life (knowledge of self) again, with self-respect and dignity (minus ego),take up his balance and reign complete (balanced) as the Creator intended. *Maat* sustained Egypt from the beginning of time, until lesser influences entered her gates, and we as a people began to look and follow these influences down into Nod. *The Book of the Coming Forth By Day* is the Kemetic story of life, its living, and afterlife. In our study of Kemetic truth we find that there is no end, there is only continuance and ascension. The cycle of four hundred years in Nod is now completed. One can continue to cycle into the *Halls of Nod*, or you can decide to *'Come Forth by Day' Into the Light;Ascension*; Maat.Which path shall you choose? How can we work together to find solutions and a clear balanced pathfor ourselves and our future selves?

A Kwanzaa Meditation
By Regina G. Ray

Look at the sun, how it shines so bright. It shines during the day and into the night when it bounces off of the moon to give us moon light. Sometimes the moon is as thin as a slice of pie; sometimes the moon light shows the whole pie. The night sky, when we can see them, is full of stars; see them flickering like little flashes or candle lights. Planets waltz around the sun day and night. The sun shines upon your face on a bright sunny day, and stars twinkle with every smile.

Look at the trees, how they stand so tall and strong. They have been there for many years, watching all who comes and goes. They're even watching you now. Trees grow green petals that float upon the wind. They wave you off to school and to work; and then they wave you back again. When fall arrives green petals turn colors of reds and yellows before they wave goodbye. They leave to fertilize the Earth's brown soil, so as they leave, don't you forget to say goodbye and wait till springtime comes around when they peek their eyes in preparation to return again to greet the sky, the sun, the stars, and the moon; and yes they return to greet you too.

Look at the softness of the earth; soft wet soil that turns to powdery brown dust or grow green grass in tufts. Bugs, animals, and all kinds of stuff spend hours at play as they roll in its green grass or dry hey. Have you rolled down the hill in summer fun, or slip and slide when the winter snows come? You should try it, I'm sure you will see how happy and fun a hill can be.From the earth pick corn, beans, tomato and greens for mom and dad to cook. Then give thanks to the Creator for the food that you took.

Now close your eyes and look into yourself; hear the quiet of your heartbeat as you breathe in and breathe out. Feel the calmness of your arms folded down and relaxed. Wiggle your toes and your nose; raise your shoulders up and down, then quietly breathe again. Let your head fall forward, side, back, to side, forward again and up. Say your name, smile and breathe, then just be still until you are ready to open your eyes again.

TIME LINE

Paleolithic	Neolithic	**	A n c i e n t A g e	Christ	Medieval Age	Modern Age	Contemporary Age
3mill. I 10000 BC I		3000 BC I	1500 BC 332 BC I 4 AD I 500 AD			1500 AD	1800 AD 1900 AD
First Kemetic	Hieroglyphic&	Monumental	Olmec, Amexum,Greece	Fall of Rome		Europe in	European Occupation
Man Egypt	Writing	Age	Civilization	Rome in Egypt,	Moors in Spain,	Americas	Native Massacres

*BC = Before Christ   *AD or AC = After Death of Christ (Roman calendar designations)
**In the Christian calendar there are 76 generations between Adam and Jesus. That is 3,974 years and represents the 2nd creation.

HISTORY OF OUR TIME IN NOD

What's special about this body of ancient knowledge is what many have come to suspect today of its origins.   Because the mainstream educational system of modern westernization teaches that humans began in a state of *'primitive'* nature, the mainstream perception is that man improves with time; that we are better today than we were at man's beginning.   This does not reflect the monumental and archeological data. From this view, man has improved upon physical comforts only, yet at debilitative costs to **Native Sons,** and**Mother Earth,** andto human existence overall.

However, those who subscribe to an eastern perception come to realize that the spiritual loss which western man suffers isdue to karmic effects.

> *The 'theme' of past and current historical writings, when studied*
> *carefully, is the slow but steady assuming and consuming of Native*
> *culture and identity by its non-native writers. Writings by the writers*
> *of his-story are out of their own heads, in their own words, and from their*
> *personal perspective. In the end, their writings biasly curtailed the details*
> *of events toward their own bias greed, beliefs, and favorability.*

Literature and the writing of history have undoubtedly been dominated by European writers from their northern homeland to this western world.That makes sense in their current controlling of western territories.

Example: *Internet article reads: "Some would say Neanderthals didn't go extinct, because everyone alive today whose ancestry is from outside of Africa carries a little bit of Neanderthal DNA in their genes." [Smithsonian, August 11, 2015. John Gibbons; www.si.edu]*

Response: *As loaded and irresponsible the statement above is, with the complete post-colonial whitening and lightening of the world, I will let you ponder the number of bias angles this and the increasing number of bias articles being published on the internet contain today.*

(Watch out for the pine cones!)

Until now, we as Native Sons and Daughters have found ourselves in cycles of starts and fits as we seek an exit from the detrimental grip of Northerners. While we are constantly focused on a narrow image of current events that distract, we have been unable to collectively unite and mount a proper response for the Native predicament. Our Native leaders ultimately marry into Northerner ranks, while our elders lead our children into Roman temples of indoctrination. Unity seems impossible, yet we must continue to work to provide an aerial view of time and the events that got us to this point. It is this aerial view by which we can find a clear view above the forest in order to plot a path out. This book is an attempt to provide the basis of the hidden knowledge so that all man and woman can have an overstanding of self, and thereby gain confidence in self to stand strong in their spiritual power and to know the true *Creator* through creation, not doctrine.

For centuries religions have been formulated by man in an effort to provide moral standards for the untamed nature of man. Humans have been designated as members of the Animal Kingdom. According to the theory of *Darwinism*, humans have been determined by the *northern scientific community* to have evolved over time from simple animals, even from single celled animals that emerged from the seas; this, however, is *the Northerner's story andview* due to the Northerner's primitive and late arrival onto the world scene. I make this distinction because when this Northern man was emerging out from the caves of Europe, Native civilizations around the world were experiencing cultural heights. While the Northerners of Europe look to 4 A.D., or later, as the height of their emergence, Native Sons & Daughters of the east were pursuing their writings, philosophies, mathematics, agriculture, architecture, metal works, tool making, musical instruments, technology, astrology, astronomy etc. from well before an since Prehistoric times.

Where is the proof of this? Native monuments, pyramids, temples, statues, documents, and artifacts are spread across the globe from east to west and in southern lands, and evidence exists from tens of thousands of years. Where writings and records of the Native story are found on engraved stone, or in cave paintings, Native 'written records' of these past times were burned and destroyed by invading Northerners wherever they so ventured. For example, approx. 391 B.C. the designated Temple of Serapis, as a small library which held a tenth of the books of Egypt was destroyed by Romans; again in 48 B.C. there was the burning of the entire library at Alexandria in Egypt again by Romans [during Greek occupation]; in the 1500s at the start of the *Inquisition*, Roman Catholic priests set ablaze 'western Native Codices'[Poole] as well as eastern scrolls. Inquisition orders continued to be exercised in the American expeditions. Wherever Northerners sought control, this was their practice of conquest.*(Refer to illustration below)*

The English language, being the last developed language, is made up of world languages that were in existence prior to its own; Latin, Greek, French, German, Arabic, Spanish, and all that it has devised or borrowed since, forms what is in use today. The Greeks were of southeastern Europe and came into contact with the ancient knowledge early. European philosophers frequented Egypt for its vast libraries and body of knowledge. They went there to learn.

up the picked bones and sold them by the carload for fertilizer.

Hunting parties were organized for sport. Noblemen from Europe, frontiersmen, and even women, rode on the buffalo chase. General Philip Sheridan and Buffalo Bill once gave a party in Nebraska for Grand Duke Alexis of Russia.

You can imagine that very soon there weren't many buffalo left.

After the buffalo were gone, thousands of heads of cattle were turned loose to graze on the prairie. Millions of sheep followed, nibbling at the remains of the grass until there wasn't a blade left.

The settlers and the farmers killed off the flocks of wild geese, the storks, the cranes, the swans, the ducks, the prairie chickens and the quail. By and by there wasn't even a wild turkey left.

Lumber companies went into the forests and

168 *

cut down thousands of feet of timber, and burned what they didn't use.

It was a great big party in the get-rich-quick spirit—the Big Bonanza.

The Indians were treated with little respect for their rights. If they resisted, experienced troops led by men like General Sherman and General Sheridan went out and "pacified" them. General Sheridan's slogan was, "The only good Indian is a dead Indian." Red Cloud, the Indian chief who had visited General Dodge, was one of the last to be put down.

The Indians who were left were herded into little reservations where there wasn't room enough for anybody to make a living. Even then they weren't let alone. If the white men found something on the reservations that they wanted for themselves—oil, for example—they got the government to move the Indians somewhere else —usually to some place even worse.

The more sober citizens in that section had

* 169

Ref; Nathan, Adele. *The Building of the First Transcontinental Railroad.* Spencer Press, Inc., Chicago,1950.

*The Caledonian pinewood forest of Europe in 5000 B.C. estimated to have covered 3,700,000 acres, now covers 44,000 acres in 35 separate remnants. Loss of vast sections of the forest prompted migrations to the Americas, where European destructive efforts continued as indicated in the above illustration.

Eastern and African Kingdoms were well established and settled for more than ten thousand years prior. Favored time pleasers were literature, architecture, science, and the arts.Commerce and trade routes of developed goods and natural resources had long become established between eastern kingdoms. The law in African Egypt was **Maat**.Maat was the moral self sustaining law that made and preserved the African lifestyle of Egypt from its beginnings. *Maat* was divinely ordained by the *Creator*.

In 332 B.C. the Greekslater invaded Egypt under its ruler *Ptolemy*. Greek rule in Egypt waslater overcome and replaced by the barbarians of Romein 30 B.C. who were illiterate. The *Romans had previously burned the Library at Alexandria in 48 B.C. during the Greek Ptolemy period. The Alexandria Library was the largest in the world. It housed over a half million documents from Assyria, Greece, Persia, India, Egypt, and many other nations. Imagine the loss of so much ancient knowledge.

When you study the writing about ancient times you can't miss the many distortions and rewritings of his-story that Northerners continue in their attempts to insert themselves into the African story; for example is the claims of Rome's presence in Egypt as early as 3150 B.C. – Jewish history uses this same method, whereas 'Israel' is modern day construct of stolen land from the Palestinians in 1948 when many European Jews were flown in by the plane full to Palestine from western Europe following WWII. This common European method in their writings of history is known as 'The Arrogance ofIgnorance' and is used as a 'path topower.' In this same way, many of the word definitions that appear at the top of web pages are very abbreviated, opinionated, and inaccurate or have been re-purposed out of their original meaning; their method of "controlling the narrative."

During the time that the northern European made his way into Egypt at the turn of the New Era (B.C. – A.D.) there was much barbarism of warring and conquering back and forth across the landscapes of Europe. Their existence was of a barbaric nature. Kingdoms were in their developmental stages. The law was 'kill or be killed.' There was much white on white slavery and many takeovers on a small scale as well as on a large scale.A description of early Europe:

> "There is nothing but constant wars. The feudal system, looking at this honestly, if you were a stronger so-called lord, and your 'posse was big, and you came upon a group of people whose 'posse wasn't that big, you could literally, and it was within your right, the law – and it wasn't written law because remember the people were illiterate at this time—it meant that you could overtake that individual's land. You could take his wife, daughter, everybody and take over and they became your slave."
>
> [Kaba Hiawatha Kamene aka; Booker T. Coleman]

Neither the Greek nor the barbarism of Rome could maintain the grandeur of Egypt, although Egypt had started its decline centuries prior from serial invasions by the Persians, Assyrians, and others.

> The greatest of the [African] Kemetic rulers was Menes of the First 'recorded' Dynasty 3150 B.C. – 2686 B.C., credited with the first re-unification of Kemet prior to the period known as the Old Kingdom 2686 – 2181 B.C. It was Mentuhotep II credited with the second reunification of the divided land of Kemet known today as the Middle Kingdom period 2030 - 1650 B.C. the Eleventh – Fourteenth Dynasties.
>
> [Ref; The Destruction of Black Civilization, by Chancellor Williams]

Many of Egypt's citizens and high priests were killed off or escaped into southern and western Africa, and into India. Life as the original citizens of Egypt once knew it had come to an end. Invading forces of long ago had entered its gates and altered its story and traditions. Greeks and Romans ventured in and out of its temples and shrines removing artifacts at will. The native citizenry had vanished, as did ancient faces and names of African Kemetic origin that first graced templeswere removed and replaced with foreign ones. In its end, many of the temple statues were defaced as Christians began to enter the gates of Kemetic cities. The traditions and lifestyles had long ago become contaminated with altered tales of confusion. African Egypt was gone.

Following the pilfering of Egypt by the Romans in 30 B.C., its monuments lay in ruin until Napoleon of France entered its gates in 1798 and continued defacing the monuments.The Great Sphinx had its nose chiseled off. Prior to and following the library burning at Alexandria, documents were transported out of Egypt into other lands. Over time manyEgyptian documents found their way into Western Europe.During the Ptolemy period, Egyptian scribes were used to translate hieroglyphic writings into Greek. Many Egyptian artifacts, large and small, have been distributed to cities all over Europe. This includes extensive papyri documents, mummies, jewelry, statues, gold, and obelisk amongst other items. Excavations of Egyptian burial sites by France and Englandyielded many funerary treasures.

After 4 A.D. the Hieroglyphic language of Egypt was no longer in use and was eventually lost. That is until 1799 when the French army found the **Rosetta Stone**. This carved stone is engraved with the Greek, and Hieroglyphic languages that made it possible to decipher and thus read the Hieroglyphic language again. The English then defeated the French in 1801 to resume the gleaning of Egypt. Since Europe's awakening, war has continued as its way of life.

Following the Greek and Roman occupations of Egypt, Europe fell into a long **Dark Age** of poverty and illiteracy. Few creative expressions or civilized advancements occurred during this period, filth and disease was rampant. Europe's Dark Ages lasted a vast period of time from 500 – 10,000 A.D. [Britannica].Europe's **Renaissance period** did not occur till the 15th – 16th centuries. What occurred in the midst of these two periods that is responsible for lifting Europe out of their seemingly never-ending Dark Age was the invasion into Europe by the Moors from Africa.

African trade routes had spread from eastern regions across Northern Africa to the Atlantic Coast. This is how the African Moors came to learn of Europe. They overstood the vast differences between the knowledge of the East and the barbarism of European life in the north. The Moor's determination to invade Europe was out of a desire to share Eastern knowledge and thereby upgrade European life to a civilized level into which they could expand their trade routes.[Kamene] The Moors came to be established in Spain. The Moors provided many advancements of civilization across Europe including architecturally sound structures like castles and temples, literacy by establishing universities, infrastructure such as sewer systems and running water.[Kamene]   The Moors ruled Spain during which time they too civilized all of Europe from 711 A.D. to 1492; 800 years.The Moors ruled all of Spain; they were not confined only to the Iberian Peninsula as northern writers contend. Moors resided and traveled throughout all parts of Europe. This is how Europe emerged from its *Dark Ages* of the 600's – 1600s;Europeans gained new found '*Eastern Knowledge*' delivered to them by African Moors.

In 325 A.D., during the **Council of Nicaea**,the Christian Bible became established by Christian bishops from northwest Europe under the rulership of*Emperor Constantine*. What is indeed interesting is that this Bible borrowed from much of the ancient Egyptian knowledge, though often written in encrypted code. Whereas many biblical stories are inconceivable, lack archeological evidence, and of obvious fiction, it has been taught to its parishioners' to be interpreted as literal and historical; and many do. With a literal view, the encrypted messages become just plain lost; yet the Bible remains one of the most comprehensive sources of the ancient knowledgefrom which it borrowed. Much of the ancient knowledge now exists in public view, but it is still beneficial to know the stories and messages contained in the Bible.

TIME LINE

Paleolithic	Neolithic	**Ancient Age		Christ	Medieval Age	Modern Age	Contemporary Age
3mill. |	10000 BC |	3000 BC |	1500 BC 332 BC |	4 AD | 500 AD		1500 AD	1800 AD
First Kemetic	Hieroglyphic&	Monumental	Olmec Amexum	Greece	Fall of Rome	Europe in	European Occupation
Man Egypt	Writing	Age	Civilization	Rome in Egypt	Moors in Spain	Americas	Native Massacres

*BC = Before Christ   *AD or AC = After Death of Christ (Roman calendar designations)

**In the Christian calendar there are 76 generations between Adam and Jesus. That is 3,974 years and represents the 2nd creation.

By the time thatEurope came torealize, in the 1500s -1600s, that the world was not flat,they have since taken to the seas and have navigated the world and have aggressively added 'claims' of eastern and western territories to their northern origin homelands. The 'claimed' territories, though, were already occupied by Native Sons and Daughters that have an ancestry of origin in their eastern and western homelands of tens and hundreds of thousandsof years.

During the mid part of the Dark Ages, in1184, Pope Lucius III of the Catholic Church sent bishops "throughout Europe and the Americas" (according to History.com) to root out and punish 'heresy.'This became known as the'**Inquisition**'and continued for hundreds of years.*(Some argue that it continued during and after the American Civil War here in America; the question is, Has it ended?)*

> *The Inquisition was infamous for its severity of tortures and its persecution*
> *of Jews and Muslims; …resulting in some 32,000 executions. [History.com]*

What alsooccurred during the height of the *Inquisition* is the burnings of all literature andbooks that did not conform to Christian doctrine. It was during this time that the ancient Egyptian knowledge that was studied in Europe went underground.

There were two separate edicts issued by the Roman Catholic Church to be carried out worldwide,1) The Inquisition of 1184, 2)Doctrine of Discovery of 1452; exalting a supposed moral authority over all human life and resulting in control, death, and servitude wherever the Northerner goes. These are two of the root sources of 'white supremacy'.

Destructive cycles can be traced to the patriarchal Christian church. Roman Christianity adopted theology from the east (minus its Coptic mysticisms) in an attempt to transfer the spiritual capital of the world from Jerusalem to Rome. Roman society now exists only in literature and secret society organizations. However, the greater societal existence of Rome that has survived is the Roman Catholic Church which remains the parent of all Christian denominations. Patriarchal eastern faiths, are direct protégés of the Christian faith as well, tied by as little commonality as a single prophet, demonstrate the same destructive tendencies as their parental source; as all denominations are inherently opposed to each other. Today, a societal necessity of Church is needed to maintain a patriarchal stronghold over the masses (sheep led astray) that feed its tills monetarily for as little as the tickling of an ear.

The Roman Catholic decree of the Doctrine of Discovery
Doctrine of Discovery, 1452

"...invade, search out, capture, vanquish, and subdue all Saracens and pagans whatsoever, and other enemies of Christ wheresoever placed, and the kingdoms, dukedoms, principalities, dominions, and all movable and immovable goods whatsoever held and possessed by them and to reduce their persons to perpetual slavery, and to apply and appropriate to himself and his successors the kingdoms, dukedoms, counties, principalities, dominions, possessions, and goods, and to convert them to his and their use and profit." -Pope Nicholas V (Papal Bull 1452)

Again, the question is, does this continue today? Native Sons and Daughters thought that the Klan, systemic white supremacy, and the police were the worst of our problems that continue into this new millennium. Overstand, that this awareness of the reality of what our struggle has been comes and goes from generation to generation due to inconsistencies in our access to maintain control of our circumstances educationally, politically, and economically in a racist system that works to keep Native Sons and Daughters off balance, distracted, and under duress.

YOUR ANCIENT AFRICAN ANCESTRAL KNOWLEDGE

"Knowledge of creation and of the Creator is not hidden.
Rather,it blossoms with time as fruit for nutrition.
In this way a gradual and orderly enlightenment develops."
[Contemplations In Blackby Regina G. Ray]

AGENDA OF PRESENTATIONS:

1. To begin, from our Ancients we have *The Cosmogony*. The Cosmogony explains the story of the Supreme Being and of creation as told by sages of the Dogon, Akan, Yoruba, Benin, and other West African peoples which details the dual nature of the Creator, the creation, and the universe.

2. We have the *Zodiac disc* from Temple of Hathor at Dendera that depicts at its center a Hippopotamus Goddess who represents fertility, known as **The Great Mother** who gave birth to the first Deities (Principles). She carries with her the feather of *Maat* as she ushers in the principles of *Truth* and *Balance* from the beginning. She is the personification of *The Triple Blackness of Space*; *The Primal Waters*from which all creation arise.

3. We have the *Tree of Knowledge*; the *Staff of Tehuti*; *the caduceus* whichhas today been chosen as the representative symbol of medical societies. The staff is a *Kemetic*emblem of the human body and represents all of the complex creative physical and spiritual elements known of it. An in depth study and overstanding of its deconstructed parts has the ability to open the mind to higher perceptions of self, your connection to the Creator, and to the creation. Its overstanding provides

the knowledge that is required to successfully navigate the physical and spiritual realms of existence.

4. We have the *Tree of Life* that is based upon a moral code for humanity; a mandala of innate and acquired faculties and attributes essential to achieve unity of the spiritual self with creation and the Creator.

5. We have *Maat*, a Kemetic deity who represents life based upon order, truthfulness, balance, justice and righteousness; She represents harmony of the universe. *Maat* is the personification of truth set up for everlasting from the beginning. *Maat* is recognized by a feather worn as her head dress or wearing the wings of enlightenment. The *Kemetic Goddess Maat* represents the original Laws and Principles of creation.

6. We have the *Asar and Aset (Osirian) Drama* which is an introduction to the representative Deities and to the encrypted messages of the revelations of life and its living.

7. Finally, you will be introduced to figures who have contributed to the progress of Ourstory, anda variety of realms and the happenings that occur in them, from the esoteric realm to the physical realm and those in-between. An overstanding of current sciences brings to light truths inherent in the ancient knowledge; we are just learning what the Ancients have known all along. *"All roads lead to Kemet."*

> **The college is invisible.**
> **The school is within.**
> **The Universe is the teacher.** [Sevan Bomar]

Throughout your exposure to the high ancientknowledge, you will discern, learn, and become seekers of the knowledge presented, as well as come to knowthatwhich exists*between*the lines; so you will come away with much more than is given. This is a time that has been long overdue. This knowledge is the enlightenment that we have kept a keen eye open for in the midst of our troubled times; likened to the beloved *Harriett Tubman* and many others who sacrificed to keep a candle lit so that others may find their way through and out of the entrapments and deceptions that others plant at our feet. It is not that everyone 'Wills' to become a *Seeker*, but if at all possible, leave no one behind who does.

DEFINITIONS

ALCHEMY; Scientific knowledge of how natural elements work together is the study of 'Alchemy.' It is the coupling of paired energies and their affinities for one another. Alchemy is at the interception of the spiritual and physical realms.

ANKH;

"The ANKH represents the first key to the mysteries of 'The Creation of Everything.' The Ankh means more than life – It is the most ancient symbol of a code of sounds and primordial deities.
All paired polar energies represented by the ANKH.

  AMN/AMNT - Hidden spark of life + its opposite

  NUN/NUNUT - Primordial unformed mass + its opposite

KU/KUKHET   - Qualities of Light + its opposite

HEH/HEHET   - Qualities of Infinity + its opposite

The Ankh has four distinct sides and one of them is the Loop (Nun/Nunet).   These four pairs were thought to be the Children of Tehuti and Maat. Both Tehuti (Vibration) and Maat (Order), and the four pairs themselves have their own forces."

[The Secret of the Ankh of our Ancestors by Amenuti Narmer, Feb 22, 2015Grandmother Africa.com]

Balance; noun; A State of equilibrium and parity; harmony.

Chakras;   Wheels of energy/transformers of subtle vital forces;   These wheels of energy forces originate outside of the body and enter at gateways that distribute their energies to and throughout the body realized as different emotions, sensations, and thoughts.   There are seven recognized chakras.   Chakras from lowest to the highest are the root, sacral, naval, heart, throat, brow, and crown. Each chakra vibration/frequency is associated with an aura of color. Chakras can be cleaned for optimal performance by exercises and diet that remove negative energies.

Chi; the life force of the creator; a pure, luminous, indestructible body, round and full, vast and boundless, like the orb of the sun. The meandering life force of the Chi follows the *Will* enhanced by the purity of sincere love.

Consciousness; an awareness of the cognitive process of thinking, minus the obstructions of errant imaginings and enshrouding *clouds of obsessions with objects, arbitrary thoughts, psychological afflictions, views, and opinions* so that only dispassionate perceptive knowledge arises. [*Cleary*]

Cosmogony; explains the story of the Supreme Being and of creation as told by sages of the Dogon, Akan, Yoruba, Benin, and other West African peoples which details the dual nature of the Creator, the creation, and the universe.

Creativeness; the initiation of the internal *Will* to do or to be;

Deity; a god or goddess of divine status, quality, or nature; one exalted or revered. A deity may be a recognized figure that is representative of a principle or virtue; a past ancestoror someone you may have a shared bloodline with. Examples are *Maat,Elegba*, or Grandma

Delusion;an acceptance of the existence of things and concepts that do or did not exist;beliefs.

Edenic; denoting a state of genesis; a new beginning.

endeavor; noun; endeavoring; verb

 Putting into motion the inspiration or desire to achieve a specific goal; internal drive.

Father; The masculine element of creation embodied in the word and the light; the infinite knowledge and power to do.

Fluidity; elements of adaptation, adjustment, evolution, and revolution in creation; fluidity must be allowed in order to adhere to the principle of polarity and change; the Creator in the 1st Aeon is unchanging, yet the elements in the 2nd Aeon is about creation and change.

God; word of German origin meaning guttural utterances; northern word for deity; any entity that has a name is subordinate to the unchanging Creator of the first Aeonwho has no name. When a Deity has a name, this is an indication that it is subordinate to the Creator; gods are creations from the mind of man, personifications of laws and principles, or ancestors from former lives.

Haile Selassie I, His Imperial Majesty (H.I.M.); Jah, Ras Tafari

On the small island of Jamaica, Rastafari evolved as a faith that scripturally identified *His Imperial Majesty, Emperor Haile Selassie I* of Ethiopia as the reincarnate of Jehovah upon his coronation in 1930.

His-Story (History); knowledge based upon European primitive perceptions of the world.

Ignorance; conscious or unconscious acceptance of a non-reality (conditioning); absent or irrelevant knowledge (un- or misinformed); mistaken reality (misinterpretation).

Justice; noun; conformity to truth, fact, and sound reason; equity; moral rightness.

Kemet; the original African name of Egypt, prior to Greek renaming.

Kemetic Language; the hieroglyphic writings of the Kemetic people.

King/Queen; (Kemetic, chi; ki)One that is most powerful or eminent of a particular group, category, or place; a blood line of heritage; gods of antiquity.

Knowledge; The state or fact of knowing; the familiarity, awareness, and overstanding gained through experience and study.

Kundalini; Root chakra energy that energizes third-eye spiritual insight or gnosis.

Law of Polarity; In order for there to be anything, there must first be two polarities, two sexes, two complementary forces, two opposites, two states of being. Between these two polar opposites exists all varying degrees of the same. In order to create experience, there must be constant change, and yet the source of all things must always stay the same.

Law of Correspondence; 'As above, so below', 'As within, so without' speaks to the relationship between the spiritual realm and material realm; both realms existing within the same trajectory but at polar frequencies. The spiritual realm vibrates at high frequency and the material realm vibrates at a low frequency. The high frequency is where non-tangible concepts within the mind exist – the god realm where the 'Will' and 'Life forces' confer. The low frequency is the physical realm; where the manifestation of the spiritual realm materializes.

Law Of Reciprocity; The Law of Reciprocity is a non-discriminating equitable force. Each being has a cosmic record of personal account that is monitored in cosmic energy; this can be stated in various ways, "What goes around, comes around," "Do unto others as you would have done unto you," or as "Karma." Biblically, this law is explained as an account that follows the generations of its violators; therefore children suffer the 'sins' of their parents.

Law of Cause and Effect; states that for every action applied to an event (exertion), a reaction of equal force occurs (absorption). This too is a universal observation and speaks to the physics of various dimensions; physical, psychological, and spiritual.

Life; noun; An unending ebb and flow of tension/contraction and relaxation; the energy of habit; a journey of chance when led by self; a journey of destiny when guided in knowledge. Life lived out in knowledge leads to the desired intended outcome of destiny and purpose.

Maat; a Kemetic deity who represents life based upon order, truthfulness, balance, justice and righteousness; She represents harmony of the universe. Maat is the personification of truth set up for everlasting from the beginning. Maat is recognized by a feather worn as her head dress or wearing the wings of enlightenment. The Kemetic Goddess Maat represents the original laws and principles of creation.

Mantra;   expressed energy in word and sound; the cognitive awareness of the origin and inherent energy in word and their meanings*(etymology; engl.);* word power

Marcus Mosiah Garvey; born 1887 in a parish of Jamaica Marcus Mosiah Garvey, a modern day Moses raised up the words of African Unity for the Black man to consider.   "Look to the East", he said, "from there your God cometh in your image."

Moor; descendants of Kemet; Inhabitants of Northern Africa; ruled in Spain 711- 1492.

Mother; the feminine element of creation embodied by the egg and Blackness; the source of all energy and matter; the possibility and infinite ability to be; the physical/metaphysical elements of manifestation

Mother Earth; a breathing viable organism who maintains cleanliness through her forces of wind, rain, quakes, and fire. There are daily reactions of growth and decay through her natural biological processes. All creatures dwell beneath the canopies of trees, mountains, waters, and sky and are subject to her laws of nature.

Mystery/Mythology; English terms; describes ancient knowledge that has African origins.

OM; in the First Aeonthe OM exists as the homogenous vibration of the subjective realm. *(Metu Neter)*. The *OM* is the unchanging (constant) quality of the Creator; Conscious infinite *Will*; Omniscient, Omnipotent, and Omnipresent.

Order; noun; a state of sound readiness.

Orientation; yourperceptive state of existence in the scheme of life and continuum of time.

Our Story; the hidden mysteries of life often masked in 'codes' and 'mythologies.'

Plate Tectonics; lithospheric plates that float over Earth's mantle independently; seismic activity occurs at the boundaries of these plates.

Principle; noun; a fundamental quality or attribute determining the nature or essence of matter.

> **Pineal**; agland that regulates essential physical aspects of spiritual functions; the cosmic gateway; [first] third-eye vision.

Realms; delineations of existence; interconnections between spiritual and physical planes.

> **Ethereal Realm**; the spiritual connection to the Creator; existence, extending from the inner-self where the soul is bound, to beyond earth's stratosphere into infinity. Your soul is inherently infinite.

> **Cosmic Realm**; the spiritual connection between your physical being and the universal planetary bodies of creation. Every person is a star.

> **Archetype**; four elements of creation; fire, water, air, earth; inherent physical nature of compatibility in reactionary energy couplings; alchemy.

> **Conscious**; consciousness; awareness; access of the God nature; subjective will; crossroad of the intellect; third eye vision; divine intervention; influential; persuasive; polar effects of experience.

> **Subconscious**; involuntary stimuli; submerged awareness; unknowingly influenced; programmed by systematic sensory rewards; development of habit.

> **Sensory**; tactile interactions between the physical life and its environment; involves touch, smell, hearing, tasting, and seeing; perception based upon queues of likes and dislikes.

Interdependent Relations of the Lower Realm:

    God Self – the father energy; absence of worldly influences; subconscious reality; pure energy of knowing; non-interference; non-influential; unaffected state; mummy state; oneness with nature; high principles at work; flow of the ebb; light of the orb.

    Inner Self – consciousness; awareness; access to the God nature; subjective will; crossroad of the intellect; third eye vision; divine intervention; influential; persuasive; polar effects of experience.

    Self – being; potential energy of the father; resultant matter and manifestation of the mother; transient evolution.

    Outer Self – exuded energy; perceived self; active working energy; environmental exposure.

    Nature –the mother energy; the original principles of the creation manifest; self cleansing; self sustaining; cycles of evolutionary replenishment.

    Environment – construct; network of interdependence; low vibratory realm; grounded mother energy; sustained by natural principles and created principles set into motion; compacted energy.

    Brotherhood/Sisterhood – recognition of kindred spirit; similar spiritual goals and affinity.

    Acquaintances– coincidental likeness; non-spiritual connection; temporary encounters.

    Antagonists – anti-spiritual influences; moral contrasts.

Physical; involuntary and voluntary synoptic excitation of gray matter, muscle, skeletal, organs, endocrine, pulmonary, and lymphatic bodily systems.

Religion;   A code of conducts and rituals based on agreed upon cultural practices and beliefs; a man made philosophical doctrine intended for the indoctrination and conformity of the masses.

Shona stone is unique to Zimbabwe. It is a serpentine stone of sediment on the ocean floor exposed to intense heat and pressure, formed over hundreds of millions of years. The stone comes in colors that range from yellow, green, purple, opal, to browns and Black. The Shona people of Zimbabwe hand carve the stone with elegant detail.[Ref; Wikipedia]

Zimbabwe was formerly known as Rhodesia while under British colonial rule. Zimbabwe gained its independence November 1965 and converted to a Republic April 18, 1980. Robert (Bob) Nesta Marley performed at its independence celebration.

The Shona people make up 80% of Zimbabwe's population. The Ndebele people populate southern Zimbabwe.

Sovereignty; Self- governing; independent; Royal rank, authority, and power.

Staff of Tehuti represents the Tree of Knowledge or Gnosis. The staff is emblematic of the human body and all of the complex creative physical and spiritual elements known of it.

States of Being; from high to low frequency order:

Spiritual → Celestial → Terrestrial → Natural Creations → Artificial Creations

Third Eye;aspiritual state and ability to escape the earthly realm into a higher realization of existence; the divine completeness of perception; wisdom; overstanding.

Tree of Life; Based upon a moral code for humanity; a mandala of innate and acquired faculties and attributes essential to achieve unity of the spiritual self with creation and the Creator.

Tree of Knowledge; Is super-imposed upon the tree of life; encodes the spiritual connections with the physical body.

Truth; Fidelity to an original standard based upon reality and actuality.

Universe; The universe is elegantly organized, and that aspect of creation could very well be linked together as one design, one thought. *[One-word = uni – verse.]*

Will; is the executive officer of the body. When the Will moves forward, the life force (Chi) follows. The life force meanders after the commands of the Will.

Wisdom; The overstanding of what is true; common sense and good judgment; typically comes with time and experience of an individual's connection with the creation; divinely acquired; imparted by the Creator; knowledge.

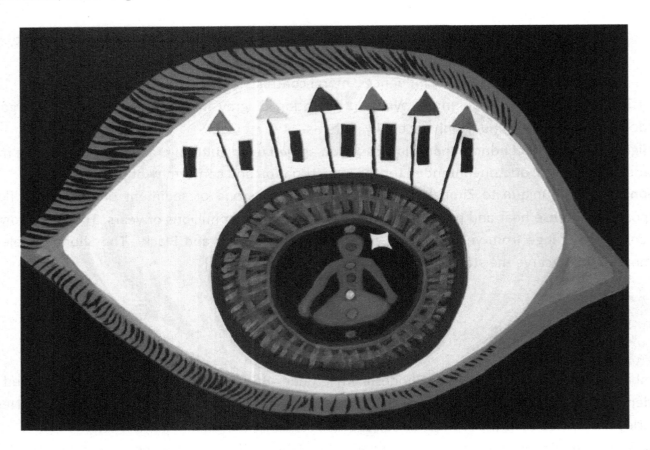

Chakras

Chakras;are wheels of energy along the vertical axis of man – the spine; transformers and doorways of subtle vital forces that originate outside of the body and distribute energy to the body as frequencies sensed by the brain as emotions, sensations, and thoughts.

Instinctively, as the living beings we are born to be, we carry on year to year observing the rise and fall of the sun with little overstanding of why. As years cross paths of life experiences we observe, wonder, and search for the meanings therein. Imaginations, hopes, and dreams queue us to the sense that something more is or should be present, and indeed there is.

As humans our physical existence is an obvious observation. What is less obvious are the energies and its expenditures that surround us internally and externally. This energy's interplay of excitation in the form of vibrations was present in the fertile seed and egg that began our fetal lives. This energy is extended to our beings through the excitations of our heart beat, but does not stop there. As blood corpuscles pulsed through our newly formed vessels our flesh and very being join with the vibrations of surrounding pulses as we join the rhythmic vibration of the universe.

At birth we break into the world with a startling shout. At death we depart the world with a withering whimper. Such is the reality of our existence, but we must overstand what happens in-between. Chakras are a piece of the puzzle in this 'between' conversation. Chakras are inclusive of and are affected by the larger system of 'The Tree of Knowledge' that encompasses the physical and spiritually associated qualities within and without humans.

Chakras mediate the energies of our fleshly being with the energies of the surrounding physical and meta-physical environments in which we dwell. Like the maximum designated voltage that a plug and outlet will allow, chakras regulate the flow of varying energy levels. We are physical beings that are fashioned by –but not limited to- the four main elements of fire, water, air, and earth. Additionally there are different metaphysical realms in which we exist. The extent to which realms a person is able to access is a function of practice in unlocking energy levels one may aspire to in the tree of life.

There are seven major chakras that extend from the root end of the spine to the top of the head. Each is attributed to the distribution of energy at specific entry points along the spine. Each vibrating chakra correlates to a representative color, organ, and virtue. Maintenance of the chakra system through special cleansing exercises and practices can enhance optimal functioning that translates into improved virtuous living.

CHAKRAS

Chakra	Location	Color	Meaning	Element
Crown	Top of head	Purple	Intellect,Unity	Consciousness
Third eye	Brow center	Indigo	Pineal,Wisdom	Light
Throat	At the throat	Blue	Truth	Sound
Heart	Center of chest	Green	Compassion,Peace	Air
Solar	Belly	Yellow	Gut, Confidence	Fire
Sacral	Abdomen	Orange	Sex,Creativity	Water
Root	Base of spine	Red	Elimination,Stability	Earth

atlantipedia.ie

The Cosmogony

From our Ancients we have *The Cosmogony*. Knowledge of the beginning can be found in the memoirs of many ancient texts. What is best known of the Creator and the first creation is preserved in the African story of the Cosmogony. *The Cosmogony* is the wisdom of African sages who held fast to the ancient ancestral knowledge of the beginning. Kept by the tradition of oral memorial, the knowledge of creation is known from the geographical areas of the Nile River Valley that includes Egypt (Kemet) in the north and Ethiopia (Kush) in the south. This knowledge spread as man spread across the continent from east into the west amongst many tribes who have never ceased to maintain the traditions and knowledge of the ancient ones.

The Cosmogony' explains the story of the Supreme Being and of creation as told by sages of the Dogon, Akan, Yoruba, Benin, and other West African peoples which details the dual nature of the Creator, the creation, and the universe.

The Cosmogony

An excerpt from The Return, by Yao Nyamekye Morris

The Dogon, Akan, Yoruba, Benin, and other West African cosmologies all begin with a similar act of the Supreme Being. It is said that in the highest Aeon the One God, who was the first God, existed without form. There was no beginning. All things were contained within this God. There was nothing which was not God. The quality of this first God did not change, was entirely pure, and had no equal. This God was inert, still and completely pure. But there could be no experience in this Aeon, and the One God desired that there should be experience and creation. In other words, he/she/it desired that there should Be. And so the One God, who was the first God, in the highest Aeon, brought a word of power into his/her/its mouth, and through it, projected forth a reflection, a double, a shadow of itself. And this pleura projected forth from God differed in that it could change. And so immediately there occurred a differentiation of the quality of the pleura projected forth from God into two quality polarities. This created an Aeon below the highest Aeon, being the second Aeon. This differentiation did not change the One God, who was the first God, that cannot change, who continued to exist in the first Aeon as before. But now was created all potential things and possibilities, because there were two contrasting polarities in the second Aeon. The differentiation created a new God in this second Aeon, who differed in quality from the first God, the One God. This new God was neither still nor inert, but capable of change. He/she/it made the thought statement that "I Am", and began to create, change, and therefore to Be. This active God of the second Aeon is what has been known as the God of creation. He/she/it is Yahweh, Jehovah, Christ, Allah, Nyonkopon, Obatala, Krishna, Osiris, Asar, Wakan-Tonka, and etc. And the narratives go on to relate that the second God, the active God, became the representative of the First God, who is inactive. He/she/it became the main God of reality in the form of an "egg" without limitation and a "word" without limitation.

This second God, the God of creation, in its first act of creation decided to split or differentiate again. This God of reality, in the second Aeon, split or differentiated again. From this second differentiation manifested the Holy Father embodied in the Word and the Light, and the Holy Mother, embodied by the egg and the Blackness. This darkness is not the absence or a void, but the great Black light, that essence which contains all light, all of the colors blended together, all potentials of being. The body of this Holy Mother, being the Great Black, the source of all energy and matter, the primal waters. Our connection to these primal waters is the great Blackness being our melanin. This egg represents the possibility of infinite creation and infinite ability to be. This word represents infinite knowledge and power to do.

The teaching goes on to relate key concepts...this second God of creation however, was always connected to the first God, and its very existence and power depended on this connection. Without this connection to the first God, who is inactive and still, the second God, who is active and causes existence, could not exist. This then is the duality that defines everything in the universe. For every real component in our world that exists and can change, there is a complementary component that exists in the actuality that has no tangible manifestation in the physical world to give evidence of its existence. Yet one cannot exist without the other. From this cosmology, and its extensions, comes the principle of duality.

The dual nature of the Creator is reflected in everything that exists in the universe. For every tangible, real thing that manifests, there is an intangible, actual thing having no manifestation, being part of the inert God, and which allows the real thing to have existence. For in order for there to be anything, there must first be two polarities, two sexes, two complementary forces, two opposites, two states of being in order for there to be anything at all. In other words, there must be something to contrast with in order for there to be change. In order to create experience, there must be constant change, and yet the source of all things must always stay the same.

Photo   photo

MOTHER NATURE – *MUT NETCHER*

In Kemet, the *Zodiac disc* from the Temple of Hathor at *Dendera,*depicts at its center a Hippopotamus Goddess who represents fertility, known as **The Great Mother** who gave birth to the first Deities (Principles). She carries with her the feather of *Maat* as she ushers in the principles of *Truth* and *Balance* from the beginning. She is the personification of *The Triple Blackness of Space; The Primal Waters* from which all creation arise.All has been born from the womb of the *Great Black* – the *Primal Waters*, into *Existence*.

> *Exist;*
> *Ex- = exit   -ist = root of sister*
> *definition; literal; exit her; come out from her.*[Linda Karim]

> *The Holy Mother is embodied in the 'egg' and the blackness… The body of this Holy Mother being the Great Black; the source of all energy and matter, the Primal Waters.* [C.I.B., The Cosmogony]

Paternal world religions refer to the presence of the Creator always as Him or He. This acknowledges the masculine aspect of the Creator. Yet, alone this is representative of imbalance.

43

The masculine energy cannot exist without the feminine energy. Both the yang and yin vibrations resound within the OM of the 1st Aeon. The 2nd Aeon is the result of a projection of the first, thus both are maintained in balance. The Creator of the 1st Aeon remains unchanged. Once established, the fertile portal for the deliverance of creation berths both the yin and yang into existence. Balance is contained within the formula of creation. This is why *The Great Mother* is seen carrying the feather of Maat from the beginning.

All of creation was born from the womb of creation and continues in the same manner. Ancient and early civilizations recognized the feminine role as an important role in creation. Both masculine and feminine energies work together; one cannot exist without the other. These complimentary energies spin in opposite directions. Opposite spins create the magnetism that binds both into close proximity as energy is created within and without. The Creator resides in the 1st Aeon. It is in the 2nd Aeon where the Creator is expressed.

Feminine energy is known as the '*manifestation*' of intellect.'*Intellect*' is a masculine energy. This speaks to the duality of creation from its beginning; each energy working together with the other. When the Principles of intellect are put forth, they manifest (take form or shape) within creation; '*As above, so below.*' The existence of the planets and all that make up the many universes are a result of 'intellect manifested.' The manifestation is spoken of in terms of 'Mother Nature," whom we acknowledge in all events of nature both great and small; in greater events such as weather patterns, and in small events such an ant nest.

In Kemetic mythology there are three significant depictions of the feminine energy;
The Great Mother
Hathor-Mut Netcher
Ammut
At the center of the Kemetic (Egyptian) Zodiac Disc from the Temple of Hathor at Dendera is a picture of a Hippopotamus Goddess who represents fertility. Known as **The Great Mother** who gave birth to the first Deities, She carries with her the feather of Maat. She is the personification of *The Triple Blackness of Space; The Primal Waters,* from which she gave birth to her first born in the Canis Constellation, of the greater Constellation of Draco, where the *Dog Star* –Sirius resides. According to the Dogon tribe, who are descendants of Ancient Egypt, they declare that the Sirius Star is their place of origin. Kemetic astronomy regards the Sirius star as the Central Sun of our universe. The **Great Mother** is at the center of creation in the 2nd Aeon.

This overstanding of the Dendera Zodiac shows that the purpose is also
to remind us of the role of the feminine principle in the process of creation.
[www.afrikaiswoke.com]

The Goddess **Hathor; Mut Netcher** is the personification of Mother Nature. She is noted in many forms. Some listed as:

Mut Netcher – Hathor; the Great Mother of the World; Mother Nature; the Great Universal Mother of the sky Goddess, and dates to pre-dynastic times as she appears on the Narmer palette; she represents the feminine principle; the Cosmic Mother; Lady of the Stars; Lady of the Universe; Mother of the Sky; Wife/Mother of Heru; Associated with the sacred cow symbol of fertility; she was celebrated at the Temple of Dendera; appears with Bast in the Temple of Kefre at Giza; remained a popular Goddess throughout Egyptian History. [ancientegyptonline.com.uk]

The third figure is **Ammut**, who sits as the devourer at the foot of the scales during the *Ceremony of Scales* in the afterlife. She awaits the renderings of verdicts from the *Council of Elders* who presides over the ceremony. For those who have been found unworthy to have their names written into the *'Book of Life'* by *Tehuti* the scribe, *Ammut* devourers the soul and the heart of those unworthy to continue on.

Ancient Egyptians often showed Ammut as a female creature with the head of a crocodile, the hindquarters of a hippopotamus, and the forequarters of a lion. [www.worldhistoryedu.com]

The science of Astronomy and Astrology was worked out from Kemet's inception as represented by the *Narmer Palette* of 3100 B.C. The *Zodiac from Dendera* from 50 B.C. is a compilation of all created knowledge that has since been revealed.

Like a carefully composed orchestrated symphony, this Kemetic knowledge encompasses all of the elements of creation; of what came first, of that which is, and is to follow. It is the story of The *Great Mother* of the *Primal Waters*; the mystery of life. She is the *Portal*; the *Pearly Gates*; the *Star Gate* between the creation and the *Creator*. It is upon her waters that all enter into life, and the waters through which our soul must earn the rights of return.

The Tree of Knowledge

The *'Tree of Knowledge'* is a complex structure represented by the *'Staff of Tehuti'*. An in depth study and overstanding of its deconstructed parts has the ability to open the mind to higher perceptions of self, your connection to the Creator, and to the creation. Its overstanding provides the knowledge that is required to navigate the physical and spiritual realms of existence.

The staff is of Kemetic origin and represents the *Tree of Knowledge* or *Gnosis*.

Bindu seed; **Pineal**
Wings of Enlightenment; **Maat**
Rod – Backbone of Man; **Spine**
Serpents; **Kundalini Energy**

Crown Chakra
Third Eye Chakra
Throat Chakra
Heart Chakra
Solar Plexus Chakra
Sacral Chakra
Root Chakra

Definitions:

Pineal-gland that regulates essential physical aspects
of spiritual functions; the cosmic gateway; third-eye vision

Maat – Egyptian Goddess; personified harmony of the universe;
represents order, truth, and justice; All humans sought to live
by her ethical rule.

Kundalini – root chakra energy that energizes third-eye spiritual insight or Gnosis.

Chakras- wheels of energy along the vertical axis of man –
the *backbone (spine); transformers and doorways of subtle
vital forces that originate outside of the body and distribute
energy to and throughout the body as frequencies, sensed
by the brain as emotions, sensations, and thoughts.

The *Staff (caduceus) ofTehuti* can be depicted as a shaft that is common to many subsequent periods and tribes. Yet, *Tehuti's* staff represents the full stature of his very being; his physical and spiritual character expressed in the very depths of knowledge into which he was immersed.

The symbol of *Tehuti's* staff has today been chosen as the representative symbol of medical societies. The staff is emblematic of the human body and all of the complex creative physical and spiritual elements known of it. This knowledge, in the latter part of mans existence has been seemingly lost in the whirl winds of time, but is now sought for the healing and perpetuation of continued life. The staff continues to carry the mind of man deeper into the depths of its mysteries.

Tehuti is known as the Kemetic Scribe of the original principles and laws of order that was set up from the beginning. He was entrusted with the task of overseeing ceremonial high courts of judgment over which an assembly called *"The Council of Elders"* presided to pass judgment upon the life of a man or woman during their transition from an earthly existence to their decided fate in the afterlife.

Tehuti is portrayed as having the head of an ibis bird. This very portrayal represents his elevated spiritual unity with the creation and the Creator. As a scribe, he is attributed to the earliest recorded wisdom and knowledge. His hieroglyphic (*Metu Neter*) recordings provided guidance for human existence in past lives, and now are a prominent source of knowledge to us today. The responsibility of Tehuti in the scale ceremony is to maintain an accurate accounting as to whose name was inscribed into the *'Book of Life.'* Such an honorable induction afforded the inductee a ride in *'The Boat of Blessing'* across the *'Duat'* (the *Abyss*) to reside with the Creator in *'The House of Blessing.'* This is the origin of the promise to man.

from
The Return by Yao Nyamekye Morris

The Tree of Life

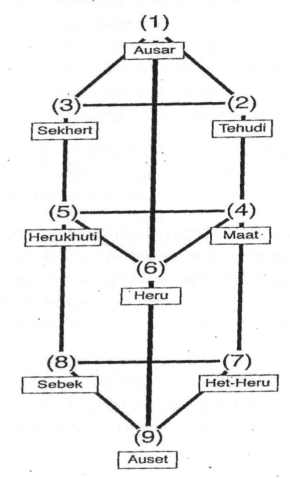

Sphere 1-6 are attributes of Higher Self

Sphere 7,8 & 9 are active at birth

Ausar	Sphere 1 Divinity	Unity. The ability to be one with all things. The "Mummy", a nature so highly evolved, one is immune to all emotional or earthy influences.
Tehudi	Sphere 2 Divine Wisdom	The ability to intuit all knowledge, directly, first hand. "All knowing." The ability to communicate with each faculty of God directly. The level of the sage.
Sekhert	Sphere 3 Divine Power	Control of the life force, the formative base of all things in the world. Governs the cycles of life and death, yin and yang.
Maat	Sphere 4 Divine Truth	The ability to comprehend the natural law. Truth is a measure of how function adheres to form. Do we live according to God's design? The ability to acquire one's needs through an understanding of the laws governing a situation.
Herukhuti	Sphere 5 Justice	The attribute of defense and protection. The use of spiritual power to defend from external attack. The use of spiritual power to heal inside the body, internal attack.
Heru	Sphere 6 The Will	The ability to rise above fears and conditionings, and exercise the will. The use of the will to live truth. The ability to self regulate oneself.
Het Heru	Sphere 7 Harmony, Beauty	The ability to get along with people and things that are different from us. The full manifestation of the seductive aspect of our sexual nature. The ability to attract, physically and spiritually. The employment of the imagination to create.
Sebek	Sphere 8 Language	The faculty that allows us to separate and define the parts of a whole. Our ability to communicate thoughts, but not the act of thinking.
Auset	Sphere 9 Devotion	The faculty of trance. Devotion. The tendency to mimic others. The nurturing instinct.

The Tree of Life

We have the *Tree of Life* that is based upon a moral code for humanity; a mandala of innate and acquired faculties and attributes essential to achieve unity of the spiritual self with creation and the Creator.

Ancient wisdom can be found in the construct of a tree referred to as a '*mandala.*' Ancient texts reference two different trees;

1) The Tree of Life
2) The Tree of Knowledge

The Tree Of Life demonstrates the progression of man/woman through spiritual stages of development from birth. Within these ancient writings is a map of pre-recorded knowledge from those who have gone before. Their recorded awareness provides an overstanding of the generalizations of life for helpful navigation.

Starting from the bottom of the tree, (stages 9-7), it is recognized that every human is born with common faculties such as instinct, communication, socialization, and imagination. Additional faculties (stages 6-2) may be acquired through increased knowledge and divine awareness. It is beneficial to have an awareness of the faculties of the *Tree Of Life*. It is even more beneficial to learn how to navigate its ascension. Together with proper training and divine inspiration, it is possible for man/woman to reach his/her highest level of consciousness, (Stage 1).

TREE OF LIFE AFFIRMATIONS

9. Aset; Devotion (active at birth)
The faculty of trance; nurturing instinct; devotion; the tendency to mimic others.

I draw upon intuitive resources for the successful completion of plans and projects. I successfully cultivate talent and abilities with purpose and work. In thought, word, and deed I rest my life upon the Eternal Being. The Kingdom of Spirit is embodied in my flesh.

49

8. Sebek; Communication (active at birth)

The faculty that allows us to separate and define the parts of a whole; The ability to communicate thoughts, but not the act of thinking. Communication is one of the three faculties through which our behavior can be reprogrammed at will. Gain knowledge to grow beyond innate instincts. Prepare to make sacrifices for the spiritual awakening of the will and the life force.

I formulate and empower mental images of success with desires and emotions that motivate me to achieve.I look forward with confidence to the perfect realization of eternal life.

7.Het Heru; Harmony and Beauty (active at birth)

The ability to get along with people and things that are different; The full manifestation of a seductive and sexual nature; The ability to attract, physically and spiritually.

In all things, great and small, I see the beauty in divine expression. I do not yield to habits and negative behaviorthat bring pain and suffering.

6.Heru; The Will

Man's will; the freedom to choose is man's greatest gift from the Creator; the ability to rise above fears and conditionings and exercise the will; the use of the will to live in truth; the ability to self regulate oneself.

Instead of following the emotional compulsions of the human mind, I choose to joyfully activate the Creator's spiritual power within.Living from that will that is supported by unfailing wisdom and overstanding.Mine is a victorious life.

5.Herukhuti; Justice

The attribute of defense and protection. Our protection from the injustices of others can only come from our beings, the vessels of the Creator's wisdom and spiritual power in the world. This is your power to immediately cut the negative thoughts and emotions that obstruct good attributes from manifesting in your spirit; the use of spiritual power to defend from external attack; the use of spiritual power to heal inside the body from internal attacks.

I identify and transform the forces and conditions that attempt to obstruct my progress. I recognize the manifestation of theundeviating justice in all the circumstances of my life.

4.Maat; Divine Truth

Because we are separated in the inferior part of our being, and united in the superior part, the emotion of unity which is love is the most powerful of all emotions. When we are able to radiate love as a spiritual force, it generates order, peace and harmony within our being and to others in our surroundings. Love is the key to peace and prosperity through cooperation and health; the ability to comprehend natural law. Truth is the ability to acquire one's needs through an overstanding of the laws governing the situation.

I attract the resources that are required to facilitate my growth and development. From the exhaustless riches of limitless substance, I draw all things needful, both spiritual and material.

3. Sekhert; Divine Power

The Creator provides everyone spiritual power in the absence of help or resources. Control of the life force is the formative base of all things in the world; it governs the cycles of life and death; yin and yang.

Filled with overstanding of its perfect law, I am guided moment by moment along the path of liberation. I perceive the vocation through which my unique energy pattern will find its highest expression.

2. Tehuti; Divine Wisdom

The Creator has made it possible to intuit its word, that we may receive direct guidance in the affairs of our lives; the ability to intuit all knowledge directly, first hand; "All knowing;" the ability to communicate with each faculty of God directly; the level of Sage.

Through me its unfailing wisdom takes form in thought and word. I am fully aware of my innate talents and abilities.

❖

1. Asar; Divinity

The spiritual center of our oneness with the Creator and the creation; absolute emotional impartiality is necessary for the realization of selflessness and transcendental peace; unity; the ability to be one with all things; the "mummy" state; a nature so highly evolved, one is immune to all emotional or earthly influences.

I am a center of expression for the primal will to do good which eternally creates and sustains the universe. All the power that ever was or will be is here now. I am a creative being with unlimited possibilities

photo

photo

The Book of *Maat*

Maat is a Kemetic deity who represents life based upon order, truthfulness, balance, justice and righteousness; She represents harmony of the universe. Maat is the personification of truth set up for everlasting from the beginning. Maat is recognized by a feather worn as her head dress or wearing the wings of enlightenment. The Kemetic Goddess Maat represents the original laws and principles of creation.

The hieroglyph that represents the *Goddess Maat* is the symbol of a feather; a place holder in space and for all times of the principles that represent the constructed foundation on which creation is hinged. Man's heart is weighed upon her scales against the feather. In this manner, the dictates of her laws are the standards by which daily life of man is measured and judged; by righteousness, justice, truth, balance.

The 'Laws of *Maat*' are the keys that unlock the doors to the highest realms of the afterlife for whosoever seeks her guidance through, and beyond the abyss. Her scales reason out the balance between life and death. The leveling that exists between these two polar opposites are the choices and compromises that are negotiated over time. Man, during the course of life, is incapable of living at either polar end and therefore must negotiate his or her steps along the balance in between.

Ever so rarely shall the heart weigh less than the feather, so that the room for error is ever so slight; minute at best. The four chambered heart of layered tissue and gristle works only when filled to capacity with discs of corpuscle afloat in weighty viscous serum. The failure of one chamber means the failure of the whole. The heart is a network of nerves shocked with impulse of powered energy second by second in its muscled tendons to uphold the uphill flow of synchronized streaming. Involuntary some say, but every choice during each waking day of life effects the success of its overall function in the life of this lower realm and thereafter.

The feather, on the other hand, in its plucked state carries next to no weight within itself. Its origin emerged as a tentacle of fluff out of the warm yolk of matured egg. Its' newly hatched host ran free across meadows of flower for its' first dive into sun lit waters. It has spent its days floating down streams of heaven sent waters, only to be blown dry by the gentlest of wind. Secured from the tail of fowl; the feather stands erect, unbound, on its own merit. Its beauty unhindered in remembrance of how simplistic life is made to be from its start.

From The Kemetic Writings:

FORTY-TWO LAWS OF MAAT

I will/have not do wrong

I will/have not steal

I will/have not act with violence

I will/have not kill

I will/have not act unjustly

I will/have not turn from words of right and truth

I will/have not utter curses

I will/have not lie

I will/have not be excitable or contentious

I will/have not desecrate holy places

I will/have not prejudge

I will/have not be an eavesdropper

I will/have not speak overmuch

I will/have not cause the shedding of tears

I will/have not sow seeds of regret

I will/have not commit treason against my Ancestors

I will/have not be an aggressor

I will/have not act guilefully

I will/have not lay waste the plowed land

I will/have not bear false witness

I will/have not copulate with a man's wife

I will/have not set my mouth in motion against any person

I will/have not be wrathful and angry except for a just cause

I will/have not copulate with a woman's husband

I will/have not blaspheme NTR the One Most High

I will/have not commit fraud

I will/have not mistreat animals

I will/have not defraud the temple of offerings

I will/have not pollute myself

I will/have not cause terror+

I will/have not pollute the earth

I will/have not speak in anger

I will/have not cause pain

I will/have not waste food

I will/have not initiate a quarrel

I will/have not speak evil

I will/have not abuse my sexuality

I will/have not waste water

I will/have not do evil

I will/have not be arrogant

I will/have not mistreat children

I will/have not plunder the dead

In her feminine state *Maat* kneels on one knee with her feather adorned arms outstretched as a shield for those who seek her nurturing protection. Her graceful demeanor warrants the décor of many a most beautiful feather. Humility falls upon the path of her every step. Mercy and compassion levitates her heart. She floats always above the waves and is shielded from the storms; till the sun shows its face again amidst hues of blue skies for ever lifting flight. Keep your eyes upon her gaze. Recite her laws day by day that, too, you may travel the path of peace without and within. Keep your eyes upon the sparrow and birds in the freedom of flight, till your night storms turn into day, because life is indeed short awaiting that final night at bay.

In the masculine state *Maat* stands as erect as a feather; unmoved from the statutes of truth, righteousness, and justice defended. The heart foot remains always forward, back straight, muscle toned arms firmly braced. A picture of strength has a beauty of its own. Keep your eyes upon his gaze. Recite the laws day by day. Truth and integrity is the seat of his throne. The rod represents the practice of defense from attack. The flail serves as a reminder that daily judgment comes from within, in preparation for that fateful day when life before the *'Council of Elders'* judge what un-reconciled remains.

Maat is the answer to the mystery of the heart. We all must earn our wings based upon our words and actions of deed. Words are predicated upon what we think. What we think is predicated upon what we learn. Our words are manifested through our actions. Learn what is true, righteous, and just. Think what is true, righteous, and just. Say what is true, righteous, and just. Do what is true, righteous, and just.

The balance between what we learn, think, say, and do becomes the holdings of our heart's content/content. When that which is contained in the heart is true, righteous, and just, the scales will indeed tilt in its favor. The earned reward shall be eternal life; the right to approach the *'Tabernacle of the Creator'*; to ride in the *'Boat of Blessing'*; to eat at the *'Table of Plenty'*; to reside in *'The House of Blessing'* with the*Creator'*. These are the original promises to man.

The Story of Asar (Osiris), Aset (Isis), and Heru (Horus)

The Asar and Aset (Osirian) Drama is an introduction to the representative Deities and to the encrypted messages of the revelations of life and its living.

The Egyptian Myth of Creation from Geb, the sky god, and Nut, the earth goddess came four children: Osiris, Isis, Set and Nephthys. Osiris was the oldest and so became king of Egypt and he married his sister Isis. Osiris was a good king and commanded the respect of all who lived on the earth and the gods who dwelled in the netherworld. However, Set was always jealous of Osiris, because he did not command the respect of those on earth or those in the netherworld. One day, Set transformed himself into a vicious monster and attacked Osiris, killing him. Set then cut Osiris into pieces and distributed them throughout the length and breadth of Egypt. With Osiris dead, Set became king of Egypt, with his sister Nephthys as his wife. Nephthys, however, felt sorry for her sister Isis, who wept endlessly over her lost husband. Isis, who had great magical powers, decided to find her husband and bring him back to life long enough so that they could have a child. Together with Nephthys, Isis roamed the country, collecting the pieces of her husband's body and reassembling them. Once she completed this task, she breathed the breath of life into his body and resurrected him. They were together again, and Isis became pregnant soon after. Osiris was able to descend into the underworld, where he became the lord of that domain. The child born to Isis was named Horus, the hawk-god. When he became an adult, Horus decided to make a case before the court of gods that he, not Set, was the rightful king of Egypt. A long period of argument followed, and Set challenged Horus to a contest. The winner would become king. Set, however, did not play fair. After several matches in which Set cheated and was the victor, Horus' mother, Isis, decided to help her son and set a trap for Set. She snared him, but Set begged for his life, and Isis let him go. When he found out that she had let his enemy live, Horus became angry with his mother, and rages against her, earning him the contempt of the other gods. They decided that there would be one more match, and Set would get to choose what it would be. Set decided that the final round of the contest would be a boat race. However, in order to make the contest a challenge, Set decided that he and Horus should race boats made of stone. Horus was tricky and built a boat made of wood, covered with limestone plaster, which looked like stone. As the gods assembled for the race, Set cut the top off of a mountain to serve as his boat and set it in the water. His boat sank right away, and all the other gods laughed at him. Angry, Set transformed himself into a hippopotamus and attacked Horus' boat. Horus fought off Set, but the other gods stopped him before he could kill Set. The other gods decided that the match was a tie. Many of the gods were sympathetic to Horus, but remembered his anger toward his mother for being lenient to Set, and were unwilling to support him completely. The gods who formed the court decided to write a letter to Osiris and ask for his advice. Osiris responded with a definite answer: his son is the rightful king, and should be placed upon the throne. No one, said Osiris, should take the throne of Egypt through an act of murder, as Set had done. Set had killed Osiris, but Horus did not kill anyone, and was the better candidate. The sun and the stars, who were Osiris' allies, descended into the underworld, leaving the world in darkness. Finally, the gods agreed that Horus should claim his birthright as king of Egypt.

[edu/cairo/teachers/osiris.pdf]

Photo   photo

Kemetic Connections to the
Sirius Star &Dogon Peoples

TheCanis Constellation, of the greater Constellation of Draco, is where the Dog Star –Sirius resides. According to the Dogon tribe, who are descendants of Ancient Egypt, their tradition teaches that the Sirius Star is their place of origin. Kemetic astronomy regards the Sirius star as the Central Sun of our universe.

That which is spiritual belongs to the Cosmic Realm; that space within the Great Black. Our Kemetic ancestors maintained a spiritual connection with the Sirius star which is twice as massive as the earth's sun, and 25 times more luminous. According to Kemetic mythology, the Sirius star aligns with the 'Belt of Orion.' As the brightest star in the sky, with a distance of 8.611 light years from earth, it can be seen in clear skies during the daytime with the naked eye. Earths' distance from its looming sun, in contrast, is less than 0.1 light years away [Ref. Britannica.com].

Sirius, in the Canis Major Constellation, is where the Great Mother gave birth in the beginning to the first deities in high vibratory state; amidst the place to where we shall return from our low vibratory existence. It has been said that "Every man/woman is a star."Our ancient Kemetic ancestors celebrated their connectivity to the creation and the Creator during an annual ceremony of the'helical' ascension of the Sirius star, the brightest star in the sky, which occurs each year in mid-Augustin the north. The 'helical rising' of Sirius is the star's first appearance in the eastern morning sky before sunrise. The Great Pyramid is aligned to this celestial event. A statue of Ra erected within the Great Pyramid received a direct illumination of the star's ray straight through the Third

Eye or pineal. This event coincides with the star's alignment to the stars in the Constellation of Orion's belt.

For Ancient Kemet, the helical rising of Sirius also signaled the flooding of the Nile River basins. The Nile's flooding is what made Kemet the most fertile land in the world. The Kemetic people had both physical and spiritual reasons for celebrating these special events.

> *The Dogon are of Egyptian descent and their astronomical lore goes back thousands of years to 3200 BC. They have known for centuries that their ancestors are descendants of a species from the Sirius star system eight and a half light years away.*
>
> *[gaia.com, October 13, 2019]*

The Dogon people live in central Mali.Their ancestors migrated from the southwest and settled in the Bandiagara cliffs of Mali that provided a safehaven from Muslim invasions that were occurring across West Africa.   They have resided in Mali since the 11th century. The Dogon continue ancestral ceremonies that they have passed down for many centuries. They are famously known for their knowledge of the movements of the Sirius star which is actually a Sun. The Sirius Sun is the greater Sun of Earth's sun, and is twice as massive. The Dogon tribe celebratesthe appearance of *Sirius B, a satellite of the larger Sirius A, every sixty years in their Sigui Ceremony. Sirius B is visible by telescope from Earth every fifty yearsas it circumscribes an elliptical path around Sirius A. Previously unknown to modern astronomers, the existence of Sirius B and its rotational path around Sirius A has been confirmed by modern astronomy. [Ref.; earthsky.org]

It is necessary to retreat deep into the continent of Africa to get back to the start of creation; from there the stars are the limit. The tale of first man begins in the stars. We know this from two sources, one being the Dogon Tribe who holds the knowledge and secrets of the beginning of time. They claim a Kemetic heritage via an origin from the Sirius star system. The information they have maintained over their many generations from antiquity is collaborated by Kemetic documentations and architectural connections that are in alignment with the Sirius star.

*Sirius B is said to become visible to the Dogon between two mountain peaks.

MOOR CRUSADERS

Much has been written about the presence of the Moors in Spain, how it came to be, the details of their occupation, and the after effects. These writings are in French, Spanish, German, and other languages. Accolades and much gratitude must be accrued to the most important English account of this illustrious and important period of world events credited to the dedication of **Stanley Lane-Poole** and his 1886 publication ***The Story of the Moors in Spain.*** Whereas much of western history at best provide accounts only in brevity or a distorted nature of the subject of the Moors in Europe, and at worse leaves voids by ignoring the subject altogether in both the educational systems and in literature. Lane-Poole fills this gap with comprehensive accuracy and sensitivity toward the details of all; who, what, how, and when involved.

The Moors are Africans, Ethiopians, Kemetics, Dravidians, Arabians, Hamites, and Kushites, Saracen; depending upon what time period one is speaking. As descendants, they are one people. This is fact, regardless of country, language, or tribal affiliation.

The original inhabitants of Arabia were not the familiar Arabs of our own time, but a very much darker people. A protonegroid belt of mankind stretched across the ancient world from Africa to Malaysia.In the course of time two big migrations of fair-skinned peoples came from the north, one of them the mongoloids, to break through and transform the dark belt of man beyond India; and the other, the Caucasoid, to drive a wedge between India,[the world] and Africa.
(Dr. Bertram Thomas, former Prime Minister to the Sultan of Muscat and Oman)

To the Kush race belongs the purest Arabian blood, and also that great and very ancient civilization whose ruins abound in almost every district of the country. [John D. Baldwin, a member of the American Oriental Society]

Mohammed Muslim Moors came from the east and across northern Africa west to the Atlantic coast*"with the ambition of bringing all mankind to the knowledge of the truth."* They conquered, converted, and swelled their ranks along the way.

The first Islamic incursion into Africa was in 640 A.D., when General Amru captured Egypt." [Lane-Poole,1886]

Moors came to control commerce across much of Africa. By them,elaborate trade routes of goods and natural resources had become established between many African kingdoms. Trade spread from the eastern regions of Africa across Northern Africa to the Atlantic Coast. This is how the Moors came to learn of the barbaric condition of Europe. They overstood the vast differences between the knowledge of the East and the barbarism of European life in the west. In addition to their Islamic Crusade, the Moor's determination to invade Europe was out of a desire to share Eastern knowledge and thereby upgrade European life to a civilized level into which they could expand their trade routes.

The Moors entered Europe through the Iberian Peninsula tobecome established in Spain.A Moorish army of twelve thousand, led by the Moorish General Tarik defeated the Goths who at the time had been the rulers of Roman Spain for a span of two hundred years.The Moors possessed a variety of valuable talents and skills; well educated in mathematics, architecture, and many business trades. They provided many advancements of civilization to the people of Spain, and introduced upgrades across Europe including architecturally sound structures like castles and temples, literacy by establishing universities, infrastructure such as sewer systems and running water. The Moor presence in Europe brought an end toEurope's five hundred years of "Dark Ages" (500 – 1000 A.D.).

Moors ruled Spain and civilized Europe from 711 A.D. to 1492; 800 years.Yet, for Spain, a very dark time loomed ahead following the expulsion of the Moors; this was the beginning of the *Inquisition* in Europe when the Roman Catholic Church sought out and severely punished those who committed heresy – not confessing and conforming to the strictly enforced doctrines of the Christian Church. Thousands were tortured, burned at the stake, and lost their lives in other grim ways; **another dark period in Europe had begun.**About the ousting of the Moors from Europe, it was later said that "Spain had killed its golden goose."

SHAKA, ZULU WARRIOR

Born as *SigidikaSenzangakhona,* later known as Shaka, grew to be tall and strong in his youth, an ideal physique to be groomed in the art of battle. Prior to 1816 the Zulu was the *Mthethwa Kingdom* ruled by Dingiswayo. Upon Dingiswayo's death, Shaka, an able body proven leader, trained as a fierce warrior, and well skilled in military strategy, took over. Shaka proved to bea fearless warrior and great King as he grew his Zulu Kingdom from less than 1500 to the largest kingdom in the region by conquering neighboring kingdoms and absorbing their members into his ranks. This continued until there were no rivals of the Zulu Kingdom. The Zulu dominated the southeast region of present day South Africa.

In the building of a fierce Kingdom during his reign, Shaka made it possible for the Zulu to mount a strong defense of their homelands from the future arrivals of Northerners to the Cape of Africa. During his brief reign more than a hundred chiefdoms were brought together into a Zulu kingdom which survived not only the death of itsfounder, but later military defeats and calculated attempts to break it up.*[South African History Online – SAHO][Howcroft, P. South Africa EncyclopediaPrehistory to the Year 2000]*

On September 22, 1828 Shaka lost his life at the hands of his two brothers and body guard in retaliation for his unusual cruelty where thousands of Zulu citizens were killed in the wake of Shaka's tantrum of grief following his mother's death.

In 1823 the Zulu tribe under Shaka had divided when his first lieutenant, Mzlilkazi, rebelled. Mzlilkazi was from the Khumalo tribe, an *Ndebele* tribe that did not migrate to the Transvaal and instead remained in Zululand. Mzlilkazi took his followers and made a powerful *Ndebele Kingdom* north of the Vaal River near present day Pretoria. After coming into conflict with the British, the Ndebele again resettled in 1890 to southern Rhodesia, a British dominated territory. The kingdom then became known as the *Metabele*.

The origin of the people of South Africa is from the *Nguni* people, who originated in the Congo basin of Central Africa. They migrated south and settled within the southern cape around 200 A.D. Descendants of the Nguni people are the *Xhosa, Pondo, Thembu southern tribes, and the Zulu, Swazi,* and *Ndebele* tribes of the Northern Cape. The Zulu Kingdom had come to occupied *KwaZulu/Natal Land* of South Africa near the coast.

After 1836 the Zulu came into conflict with arriving Europeans to the southern African coast, such as the Dutch (known now as the Afrikaners), then the German Boers.

The Zulu'sfinest hours against the invaders was a successful battle during the Anglo-Zulu War against the British on January 22, 1879 at Isandlwana in Zululand when 20,000 Zulus attacked a British camp of 1,750 men *"using their traditional tactic of encirclement known as the izimpondozankomo ('horns of the buffalo')."*British reinforcements were instructed to resume the orders of their field task, and thereby unknowingly missed an opportunity to return to camp to be of assistance in ending the Zulu attack. Over 1,300 British lay dead in a field of blood.

In the twentieth century the Zulu eventually fell under the domination of the British discriminatory policies of ***apartheid***.

PRESIDENT NELSON MANDELA

Nelson Mandela was bornJuly 18, 1918 in the southeast South Africa village of*Mvezo*, into a royal family of the *Xhosa-speaking Thembu tribe*where his father Gadla Henry Mphakanyiswa (1880-1928) served as Chief. His mother, Nosekeni Fanny, was the third of four wives.   He was raised in the village of Qunu. His birth name is *Rolihlahla*, which means 'shaker of the tree.'

Mandela became active in the *African National Congress*anti-apartheid movement in the early 1940's. He was arrested and banned several timesby the South African government for his participation in the protest of unjust laws. Mandela opened his own Law office in Johannesburg August of 1952. A treason trial against him began in 1958. Nelson represented himself in his own defense. The court was mesmerized by his eloquence of speech, strategies, and overstandings of the law. The trial continued until March 29, 1961, ending with a verdict of 'Not Guilty.' Mandela went underground directly after his release.

Mandela was captured again August 5, 1961 for a political offence and sentenced to 5 years with the possibility of parole. Hewas sent to *Riker Island CorrectionalFacility* in South Africa as a political prisoner. His five year sentence dragged on to include 27 years of his life. The South African government under President de Klerk released Nelson Mandela on February 11, 1990 due to international pressures of embargos placed upon the government. Mr. Mandela was awarded the Nobel Peace Prize on December 10, 1993 along with his adversary,*Prime MinisterFrederik Willem de Klerk,*who was responsible for Mandela's imprisonment, and whom during the time of his served sentence, Mandelahad won over as a friend.

On April 27, 1994 Nelson Mandela cast the first ballot of his life in South Africa's first *one-man-one-vote* democratic election. It was a joyous occasion for the Native Sons and Daughters of South Africa. April 1994, Mandela became President of South Africa; May 10, 1994 he was inaugurated.After nine decades, the end of apartheid rule had finally come.

Nelson Mandela's life is an example of enduring faith in the Creator. Prior to and following his successful election campaign, many South African native born, young and old, bravely gave their lives to the fight against the barbaric European system of apartheid, for a civil life of freedom in their own homeland. You can read about the entirety of Mandela's life in his autobiography *Long Walk to Freedom.*President Nelson Mandela served from 1994 – 1999.

Spouse: Evelyn Mase 1944 - 1958
             Winnie Mandela 1958 – 1996
             Greca' Machel 1998 – 2013
Fathered: Six children; had 17 grandchildren, and 14 great grandchildren
Died: December 5, 2013 in Johannesburg, South Africa
Mandela's funeral was attended by the U.S. President, Barrack Obama and dignitaries from around the world.

THE OM

In The First Aeonthe OM exists as the homogenous
vibration of the subjective realm. (Metu Neter)

The *OM* is the unchanging (constant) quality of the Creator; Conscious infinite Will; Omniscient, Omnipotent, and Omnipresent. Within its being was a desire to create change. As a thought, it summoned time to arrive. When thought gave birth, time came. The Big Bang of time came as a rapid expulsion of energy into three hundred and sixty directions times infinity. This bang quieted to a whimper of the vibration of the *OhM*. This was the Second Aeon. The *OM* is the symbol for the sound of creation which never ceases. Out of it emerged creation.   Matter is simply energy in very slow vibratory motion. Energy is matter in extremely fast vibratory motion. *OM* is the word which is the Creator. Within its vibrations, everything is contained.

"The universe is elegantly organized, and that aspect of creation could very well be linked together as one design, one thought." [Blackness, by IM NUR]

[One-word = uni – verse.]

That one word is *OM*. The *OM* is described in detail in Hindu traditions and scripture.

> O = the father energy; the thought; the intellect
>
> M= the mother energy; the manifestation of thought

These two energies work together in the schemes of creation, yet all originate from the Creator in the first Aeon. *OM* is the underlying vibration of every utterance and everything that is. The sound that precedes the hum of the first note of a song, the *OM* is there. Prior to the hum was the thought of the hum that would soon expand into sound, the *OM* is there. *OM* is the vibration of the thought of the hum. Even when sound is present, and when sound has finished, the *OM* too is there. The *OM* was and is ever-present.

A KWANZAA LIFE

To have new life, you don't have to die to live anew. Make plans to accomplish your true purpose. There are many choices; much work to be done. Go and accomplish something new. Let nature be your inspiration. Stand barefoot on the grass, open your arms to the sky, breathe in deeply and proclaim "It is done!"

Open the gates to new life. Continue on to new heights. As you are guided along the roads that lay ahead, welcome the crossroads that approach at the horizons. All the knowing, and all the doing is the way to create more to know. The gates are open. You are new, fresh, and expectant of that new thing that is for you.

Breathe, smile, connect your new self to the stars above. Draw in new energies. All is new to you; new faces, new streets, new trees, new food, a new bed to sleep upon; what do you choose for new life? Go and live again. Introduce your new self to others.

Cut your losses early. Thirty years in; do not stop till you are thirty years out. Ten years in; means ten years to recovery. One year in; is a good reason to cut your losses early. Get out. Live again.

Locate your spiritual path in life.
Live in Truth, Love & Prosperity.
Fulfill the purpose for which you were created.
Learn knowledge.
Work toward your goals.
Live in Divine Power & Wisdom.

MARCUS MOSIAH GARVEY

Born 1887 in a parish of Jamaica Marcus Mosiah Garvey, a modern day Moses raised up the words of African Unity for the Black man to consider.

"Look to the East", he said, "from there your God cometh in your image."

Then arose the Black God, manifest upon the earth out of The Land of the Blacks, Ethiopia. 1930 H.I.M. Haile Selassie I rose to sit upon the Throne of King David and King Solomon recorded in the Bible. Every dignitary from around the world from Churchill to Nkrumah attended his coronation.

A humble servant named *Robert Nesta Marley* thus followed, out of the depths of Trench Town, Jamaica singing songs of love and praises to the God on earth. The Emperor in his royal jet flew to visit Island of his devotees on April 21, 1966, and later a representative delivered *H.I.M.*'s golden ring of The Lion of Judah to Bob who faithfully wore it until his final days on earth.

69

The Prophet and the Prophecy

Look To Africa!

*"Look to Africa, where a Black King shall be
crowned, for the day of deliverance is near"*
-- Marcus Garvey

Rastas echo the theme of the late *Marcus Garvey*, "Look to Africa." Those in the west who look toward Christianity look toward U-rope. Christianity through the auspices of Europe means that one look toward Europeans as the keepers of the God-head.   The English translation of the Bible was presented to the western world. This same Bible became the basis used to justify the ideals and principles of white supremacy.   Along with this European version of Christianity came the assumption of inferiority upon all dark complexion peoples of the world. It is there where African identity is lost.   Therein lays a subconscious inference of mediocrity and servitude to the world concerning the African. "Look to Africa" was the prophetic cry of modern day *Marcus Garvey*, and for good reason. Look now toward the east and every question you have ever pondered about self is answered. Look toward the east to see the light of creation. See the fulfillment of hope, truth and enlightenment. Find life more abundant and everlasting. Find self and you find the Creator, for the God-head came by you, the African, and is with you even this day. *Marcus Garvey* and his fellow Jamaicans held fast to this truth. They recognized the subversive philosophy of the europeanized African heritage. Garvey was heralded for his belief in self and for his bold determination to be heard. "Look to Africa: Garvey proclaimed. In the east we find the exceptional truth of the African story. It is there that we find our forefathers as the origin of hue-manity. It is there we find the pyramid builders. There too we find that the God-head began with the African.

"If the white man has the image of a white God, lethim worship his god as he desires. If the yellow man's God is of his race let him worship his God as he sees fit. We, as Negroes, have found a new ideal.   Whilst our God has no color, yet it is human to see everything through your own spectacles, and since the white people have seen their God through white spectacles, we have only now started our (late though it may be) to see our God through our own spectacles.

The God of Isaac and the God of Jacob let Him exist for the race that believes in the God of Isaac and the God of Jacob. We Negroes believe in the God of   Ethiopia, the everlasting God – God the Father, God the Son and God the Holy Ghost, the One God of all ages. That is the God in whom we believe, but we shall worship Him through the spectacles of Ethiopia."
– Marcus Garvey

"We have gradually won our way back into theconfidence of the God of Africa, and He shall speak with the voice of thunder, that shall shake the pillars of a corrupt and unjust world, and once more restore Ethiopia to her ancient glory."
—Marcus Garvey

Marcus Mosiah Garvey was born August 17,1887 at St. Ann's Bay on the northern coast of Jamaica. He was born to *Malcus (Marcus) Mosiah Garvey,* a mason and *Sarah Jane Richards*, a domestic servant and produce grower. He was a British colonial citizen and received education at the Church of England School in Jamaica. He later audited courses at Birkbeck College in London, 1914. His employment included printer, journalist, and publisher. He was a master orator. His accomplishments reached international proportions:

Founder of UNIA in Jamaica, July 1914

Formed a branch of UNIA in New York City, May 1916

Incorporated his business in New Your State, June 1918

Started the Negro World Newspaper, August 1918

Started the Black Star Line Shipping Company, 1919

Started the Negro Factories Corporation Plan, 1920

Announced the Liberian Colonization [Repatriation] Plan, 1920

Sends the first delegation to Monrovia, Liberia, 1921

Toured the Caribbean and Central America, 1921

Was arrested and indicted on mail fraud charges, 1922

Met with the Acting Imperial Wizard of the Klu Klux Klan, causing a backlash of opposition from Black leaders in 1922

Appealed the mail fraud charges,1923

Sent a second delegation to Liberia, 1923

Started the Black Cross Navigation &Trading Company to replace the defunct Black Star Line

Purchased the Smallwood-Corey School ("Liberty University")in Claremont, Virginia

Was imprisoned February 1925 to November 1927 in Atlanta, Georgia on mail fraud charges

Was deported from America December 1927

Toured Europe in 1928

Became proprietor of Edelweiss Park, a social center for Blacks in Kingston, Jamaica

Published Black Man 1929

Published the New Jamaican 1933

Became bankrupt, moved to London 1934

Taught at the School of African Philosophy to UNIA leaders in Toronto, 1937

Suffered a cerebral hemorrhage January 1940

Died June 10, 1940 in London, England

"If I die in Atlanta my work shall then only begin, but I shall live, in the physical or spiritual to see the day of Africa's glory. When I am dead wrap the mantle of the Red, Black, and Green around me, for in the new life Ishall rise with God's grace and blessing to lead the millions up the heights of triumph with the colors that you well know. Look for me in the whirlwind or the storm. Look for me all around you, for with God's grace, I shall come and bring with me countless millions of Black slaves who have died in America and the West Indies, and the millions in Africa to aid you in the fight for Liberty, Freedom, and Life."

– Marcus Garvey -

Marcus Mosiah Garvey was survived by his wives

Amy Ashwood (1897-1969), co-founder of the UNIA in Jamaica, journalist, feminist, playwright, and business manager of the UNIA offices in Harlem, N.Y. 1919. They were married 1919-1922

Amy Jacques (1896-1973), legal assistant in Jamaica before migrating to U.S., where she became business manager and personal secretary to *Marcus Garvey* in 1920, associate editor of the Negro World 1924-1927, and Garvey's unofficial representative during his incarceration in 1925-1927, published Philosophy and Opinions, published in 2 volumes, 1923 & 1925. They were married from 1922-1940 and bore two children, *Marcus Garvey Jr.,* in 1931 and *Julius Winston Garvey* 1933. Born in Jamaica, both are now U.S. residents.

A KWANZAA MOMENT:

Heru On The Horizon
by Regina G. Ray

Heru-em-Akhet, Ra of the Rasta Plateau stretches across the desert floor as a posthumous feline.

Guard's monumental and burial sites of our

Fathers and Queen lines.

Poised sky high under Kemet sun for all eyes to see,

Paws, with Pharaoh-like head erected before 5,000 B.C.

What do his eyes tell? What speaketh his lips

throughout all these millennia?

Created by Atlantian-LeMoorian descendants

and Kush kings of Ethiopia.

Heru on the Horizon.

The OLMEC

The Olmec, as the first Mesoamerican civilization, date to 1500 B.C. The heartland of their developments occurred in Veracruz, Tabasco, and along the Gulf of Mexico. The most detailed excavated locations are in San Lorenzo, and in La Venta. Over time the Olmec culture expanded from current Central Mexico down to Costa Rico, although their influences can be found beyond their cultural borders.The Olmec built large earth and stone pyramids. Many artifacts of jade serpentine sculptures, and stone carved altars have been excavated. The Olmec had an "extensive pantheon" of gods of *supernatural that combine features of the animal world with those of humans, blending them into each other in bewildering complexity.*"The Olmec carved stone monuments of large head figures out of basalt stone that vary in height from five to nine feet tall and weigh over 20 tons. These colossal stone heads are *portraits of Olmec rulers, their faces with thickened lips and flat noses.*" The Toltec, Mayan, Inca, and Aztec were most likely akin to or descendants of the Olmec people who initially came to inhabit the region."

The best known examples of native built mounds exist in the United States. Man-made hillocks are scattered in the thousands from the Alleghenies to the Missouri River, and from the Great Lakes to the Gulf Coast. A century ago, many scholars regarded them asa 'Race of Mound Builders', since they regarded American Indians as too uncivilized to have been capable of erecting them. However, archaeologists have long since demonstrated that mound building was, indeed, carried out by prehistoric Native Americans, though their activity was not confined to a single ethnic group or period of time.

Of interest are the similarities between the ancient civilizations found in the Americas and those on the African continent, by which we can deduce a likely association between the two continents in the distant past during a time when the continents were joined; prior to *continental drift*. Geographical stories of Atlantis that joined the Americas to Africa may account for the continental associations.

BUDDHA

Buddha was of African descent as indicated by his pepper corn hair and melanation in ancient paintings.Buddha means 'one who has awoken.' In literature by Northerners,illustrations depict *'all white faces' of the famous Native philosopherand his attentive Native guests. Buddha has inspired peace to many through the ages. 'Buddha' is a title given for one who has overcome the vanities of

this physical realm.   He provides inspiration *"tothose trapped in the endlesscycle of rebirth"*; althoughthe cycle need not be endless. Proper knowledge can initiate an intervention that breaks the cycle, thereby raising one from their subconscious state into the enlightenment of *'nirvana.'*
Vampirism: assuming and consuming the culture and identity of Native Sons & Daughters
by Northerners for cultural, economic, and political control.
Gautama Siddhartha 563-483 B.C. was a prince born into all the comforts and luxury the world had to offer. As he grew older, he insisted on venturing beyond the gates of the compoundthat offered sanctity as a shield from what lay beyond. Upon Gautama's decision to venture out on a journey, he became aware of the sufferings ofthe people of his land. Disturbed by what he had seen, he then decided to leave his family to search for the truth and purpose of his existence. Gautama found the world to be quite large and came to realize that the search for truth comes from within. He settled under a tree in meditation. There he tarried in meditation for days and nights. In this way truth was revealed as he attained enlightenment, becoming known as the Buddha. Buddha came to entertained many sojourners who sought him out for his inspiring words. He was the first to teach *"a kinder faith that respected all living beings."*

Northerner literatures present the Buddha as a religion – thus labeled as another *'schism'*, i.e. *Buddhism.* This view is through the lens of the northerner who assumes that all sees life the same as they. Buddha expresses honor and respect to the ancestors, the Creator, and to self; this is a common eastern view. There is no requirement of 'hierarchy of man' nor of 'idealized doctrines.' Buddha inspires a journey for the quest of 'self'; for one to seek their path to their higher self, while giving honor and respect to the creation that surrounds, that seeks the same.

NOBLE DREW ALI

Born January 8, 1886Noble Drew Ali is a pioneer whowas amongst the first on the political scene as an advocate for Moorish Americans. In 1913 Ali founded the *Canaanite Temple* in Newark, New Jersey. In the mid 1920s Ali had established temples and followers in Pittsburgh, Philadelphia, Washington D.C., New York, and Detroit before relocating in Chicago 1925. There he established Temple No. 9. Ali published and distributed the *Holy Koran of the Moorish Holy Temple of Science* and the temples were renamed *Science Moor Temple to reflect their evolutionary spirit.*

Central to Ali's philosophy was the importance of racial identity. In his opinion, the lot of the Blacks in America was the result of their inaccurate knowledge of themselves. Moreover, once Blacks gained a proper understanding of who they were. He believed both salvation and victory over their oppressors would be obtainable. He thus urged his followers no longer to recognize the racial designations given to them by Europeans and to call themselves Moors, Moorish-Americans, or Asiatic.*[Ann Brown, The Mogoldum Nation, 2019]*

Nobel Drew Ali possessed a keen overstanding of political arrangements occurring across the country. His formation of the temples in 1913 was based upon this keen insight. Prior to 1861 (the start of the Civil War) the formation of the country was not as it has since been presented in public education. This country started with an organic government of the *United States Republic*, agreed upon between the Natives, Moorish Moslems, and the Christians; this was under the first constitution and congress. The Native Moors had previously resided in the Americas alongside and amongst other tribes of Native populations. Other Moors, like Europeans, migrated from Spain following the start of the *Inquisition* period. Europeans of the Jewish faith,and Christians came also to escape persecutions going on in Europe. You see, history speaks only of colonist because history has been written only by colonists and their descendants. The inclusion and roles of all other populations are as the European migrants wished to present them, to European migrant advantage, and to Native demise. Nobel Drew Ali was keen to the dynamics concerning the making of America and to the political arrangements being carried on in his day.

Following the Civil War, a *Freedmen's Bureau* was established 1865 to serve the needs of the newly emancipated slaves during *Reconstruction period*. Many African Americans were elected to state legislations across the south. The state of North Carolina drafted legislation for 'White Independence' November 8, 1898. Two days later a coup followed called the *Wilmington coup and Massacre* when as many as 60 African Americans were killed in a murder spree by white supremacists protesting the participation of Blacks in the government. They then began to enact *Jim Crow* legislation that disenfranchised Blacks for many decades to come. This is the state of the country into which Noble Drew Ali was born.

At the federal level, in 1913 all Alloidal land titles were converted to Feudal Deeds and mortgages, as all properties then became hypothecated. The Europeans were converting the organic United States Republic into the samefeudal system that they had fought against in the American/British *Revolutionary War*.   This land conversion was a strategy in an effort to continue a form of profiteering from the newly emancipated peoples. Noble Drew Ali set up the *Canaanite Temple* in 1909 to preserve the people's estates. He believed that with proof of membership as a Moor, the newly emancipated would move from under a non-title to a political nationality with status, and thereby be able to hold Alloidal land title.

Noble's courageous efforts were indeed a fulfillment of his name. He was able to both read and respond to the quickly changing times. In search of his bios, I often could detect the underwhelming tone of the writer, and their rash desire to focus not on accomplishments and the obvious positive profile of character and genius. As a son of slaves, should not a man protest the lowly slot that another wishes upon him; is the education deprived not expected to seek out how to write his own books; is the disenfranchised not suppose to vote for improved recognition and representation, to organize, and make strides toward their own improvement?The enemy of aspiration, *white supremacy*, is not of a supreme status at all in all of the horrid unbecoming barbarism that no white starched shirt, bow tie, and wig can hide.

Noble Drew Ali and the *Science Moor Temple* is the primary advocate and archive for the story of African descendants prior to, during, and following the first northerner migrationsonto the shores of the Americas.

ELEGBA, LORD OF THE CROSSROADS

Subordinate Entities: The unchanging Creator of the first Aeon has no name. When a Deity has a name, this is an indication that it is subordinate to the Creator; gods are creations from the mind of man; personifications of laws and principles; or ancestors from former lives.

Deities (Gods) serve as *representations* of principles, qualities, or character. They are place holders in time. Deities are creations of grey matter in man's attempt to articulate significant representative experiences.The same quality or character of Deity may exist by different names based upon what faith or culture gives it recognition. For example, the '*Christ*' quality is recognized across almost every faith as; *Wakkan-Tonka, Asar, Osiris, Krishna, Obatala, Nyonkopon, Allah, Muhamed, Jehovah, Yahweh, Brama, Satan, Jesus, etc.*

Journey requires the expenditure of risk coupled with defiance from death – [the Will to live.] Paths twist and churn at every option, requiring decision. These are the crossroads where the chakras of the heart and gut intersect. Energies surge in all directions. Rays of energy produce the options of chance. Chance drives the fluidity of change. The resultant surge excites synoptic exchange to create the sense of sudden flight at the very moment of required choice. In this eleventh hour, time opens a window of brevity within a tense moment of stagnant limbo. Hidden paths are made visible. What force moves? What paths revealed? Which road to choose? The weight between relief and benefit motivates selection. Time is of the essence.

In this illusion of choice, you must find new strength of courage as you become transported into a dimension of refreshed newness. Yet, unknowingly, your journey ends as fast as it began as the next crossroad approaches at the horizon. The winds of change are perpetual as they deliver the rewards and consequence of possibility.

Meet *Elegba, Lord of the Crossroads. Elegba* is an ancient African *Yoruba*deity. As a guardian, protector, and communicator through divination he guides the fate of man/woman who approaches the crossroads of life. For those who are well meaning, *Elegba* provides safe passage. To those who seek mischief, he accommodates with confusion and discipline. As *Elegba* is sometimes referred to as a trickster, a sojourner does well to approach with caution. Recognize when you find yourself at a crossroad and consult your ancestors that all may go well.

PRESIDENT OBAMA & FAMILY

Elected 2008 *as U.S. President Barrack Hussein Obama,* a U.S. citizen, and of direct Kenyan descent via his father, President Obama took up residence at 600 Pennsylvania Avenue in the White House, the Presidential residence of the Nation. He was elected in the midst of the housing economic crash which required of him to become the '*Savior of the Nation'*and to pull the Nation from the brink of economic destruction. He was the right man for the job, even in the face of fierce political and racial opposition.It is believed by many that Obama is America's first African American President. This belief is based upon the U.S. color code that selectively does not recognize the African heritage of several of our earlier presidents.

As I grew up watching the centuries riddled with the bullets of assassinations, imprisonments and killings in black communities, ugly integration battles, strategic public inhibitions, civic routings and institutional discriminations against black people of America. Young people today are little informed, and that is what the northerner counts on, us forgetting, then doing it again to the next generations as if it has never happened already before; continuous deprivation and terrorism. I remember and shall not forget. I am so happy to disclose its ugly effects upon a young mind, watching it continue into adulthood, but in its stead I choose to not waste my time. I choose rather to carry the lamp of enlightenment that Harriet Tubman carried, shining an alternate route away from the evil.

Concerning the media, memories both during and post coverage of President Obama, was both endearing and disturbing. Endearing in the way in of the enthusiasm of the fulfillment of hopes; disturbing in the racially charged attacks by white people at his presence. Media coverage wasin weighing both sides, yes there was equal weight given, but how appropriate can that be when we are speaking about the most brilliant mind of modern times available to save the country; one who was required to take on the entire world of racists during the U.S.'s second depression with only a handful of serious back up people at his side. I won't' dwell. I will point out a couple of acknowledgements that we as black folks who are required to navigate daily the dangerous shark infested waters of America should have awares of:

1. As Chris Rock so elegantly points out in his special way, to be Black and 'make it' in America you must be twice [if not ten times] better, and you must grow wings [our spiritual power] and soar. Obama did this.

2. Obama came with a package so thick, it was like those German pocket dolls; every time you remove the top of the outer doll, another doll pops out. Pres. Obama had the brains, the killer good looks, the height, the swag, the outstanding wife, the beautiful children, and Grandma. He couldn't lose if he tried. I am so thankful for him given the constant attack that he endured from the start and throughout his presidency. He handled it with the grace and tenacity that his future colleague, Ketanji Brown Jackson of recent did in her historical Supreme Court hearings held before the Senate.

3. In addition to constantly having to tread through ill- infested waters, yes you guessed it; he had to fight his own people; from Jesse to Travis. It was to be expected, but we always hope for the best, that Negro minds will improve if not at least hold back.

TIME TABLE OF EVENTS of How We Got Here

King George III &*Queen Sophia Charlotte(mulatto)* of England and Ireland 1760-1820
The First Continental Congress, Philadelphia Sep 5-Oct 26, 1774 made up of 35 Moors and 20
Europeans from the original 13 colonies in protest of the British Parliament
The Articles of Association 1774

The Second Continental Congress May 10 1775,meet in Philadelphia

George Washington made Commander & Chief of the American Army 1775

Creation of American 'Family of Nations'Natives, Moors & Colonists

Declaration of Independence signed July 4, 1776

Articles of Confederation adopted/ratified 1777/1781

Revolutionary War against the British and King George III 1777

Articles of Confederation ratified March 1, 1781

First American President John Hanson, from the State of Maryland was the first to use the 'Great Seal' of the U.S. on September 16, 1782 giving George Washington, Commander of the U.S. Army, the authority to exchange British prisoners of war.

Congress met in Independence Hall in Philadelphia until 1783

1783-1790 Congress met in different cities

Congress meet in New York 1785

Preamble (Summary of Intent of Constitution) 1787

Native Continental Congress Convention, Philadelphia 1787

Naturalized Congress of the United States,
met in New York March 4, 1789

Federal Hall as First US Capitol Building New York

George Washington appointed as next US Pres. New York 1789

Second Constitution ratified by *'Colonists only'*(Adopted and Framed)
March 4, 1789

Assembly of the US Naturalized Congress & Supreme Court met in New York

US Bill of Rights drafted New York

G.W. 2nd Term in Philadelphia 1792

Washington DC becomes US Capitol City 1800

France & Napoleon invade Egypt 1798 – 1801

Democratic Party founded 1828

Republican Party founded 1854

Trail of Tears 1830-1850

Whig Party founded 1834-1856

United States Republic Coupe d'etat 1861

United States Corporation Service Company Formed in France 1861

Gold Standard Eliminated 1861

Civil War 1861 - 1865

Proclamation of Emancipation signed by Pres. Lincoln Jan 1,1863

Many Southern Black Congressmen Elected to Washington

Freedom Bureau open1865 – closed down 1870

Republican Party Pres. Lincoln Assassination 1865

Berlin Conference for European Colonization of Africa 1885-1887

US Reconstruction 1887

Draft of White Independence Nov. 8, 1898/Wilmington, NC white supremacists *coup d'état* against
elected Black Americans Nov. 10, 1898
Canaanite Temple by Noble Drew Ali & Marcus Garvey 1909
Jim Crow1900, Niagara Movement 1905,
NAACP, NY, Conference 1909
Noble Drew Ali's Conference in Cuba 1909
Formation of U.S. Shell Corp. in Puerto Rico 1913
Clear Alloidal Title to property Elimination 1913
Noble Drew Ali Nationalized U. S. Republic
to Preserve the 'We the People' Estates 1913
WWI 1914 - 1918
Marcus Garvey UNIA branch opens in New York City May 1916
White Race Riots (against the progress of African Americans) 1917–1923
The "Red Summer" of Riots &Lynchings 1919
Alcohol Prohibition 1920 –1933Roaring Twenties 1920-1929
Collapse of U.S. Shell Corp in Puerto Rico 1929
Tulsa Oklahoma / Black Wall Street Destruction 1929
FDR announces U.S. Corp. Bankrupt & Dissolved March 9, 1933
Restructuring of U.S. Shell Corp in France July 5, 1933
United States Corporation seeds all assets to the United Nations
European Colonialism Wars in Africa – 1889 – 1979
Haile Selassie I, Emperor of Ethiopia, ascends to throne of the
Solomonic Dynasty Nov. 2, 1930
WWII 1939 - 1945
Castro to power in Cuba 1953, Jamaica Independence 1956
Vietnam War 1955 - 1975
Civil Rights 1958
Republican Party Southern Policy 1961

Article:
THE SOUTHERN STRATEGY

*Black men and women who claim to be conservatives and therefore have become members of the American Republican party are clearly confused and are being exploited due to their confusion as the Republican party claims credit for ending slavery under AbrahamLincoln. Black people, please learn about the **'Southern Strategy' of 1964**.*

Once President Lyndon B. Johnson (Democrat) signed the Civil Rights Act of 1964, he stated "I think we just delivered the South to the Republican party for a long time to come." Following this the South went from a largely Democratic region to the primarily Republican region of today. Here's how:

After the Civil War, the Democratic party in the south was in opposition to Republican Reconstruction legislation. The Democratic party of the south was instead in favor of the restoration of white supremacy. In 1948 when President Truman, a Democratic, introduced Pro-Civil Rights legislation, a faction of the Democratic party deserted the party. They called themselves 'Dixiecrats' and attempted to form a third party with their nominee as Strom Thurmond, a strong opposer of Civil Rights. Although Strom Thurmond lost the election to Truman, the 'Dixiecrats' was the start of an erosion of the Democratic party. When the Texan Democratic President Johnson signed more Civil Rights legislation following the assassination of President John Kennedy, southern desertion of the Democrats to the Republican party became complete. Conversely, African Americans, previously Lincoln Republicans, began to sign onto the Democratic party. There was a total flip flop of party membership. Today the Republican party is comprised of the former Dixiecrats that are anti-Civil Rights and anti-Immigration (selectively). This ignorance of facts by African American Trump supporters is readily exploited by Republicans in search of all the votes that they can muster just to get into office to continue their Dixiecrat agendas.

[How the Party of Lincoln Won Over the Once Democratic South
by Becky Little Aug 18, 2017/Apr 10, 2019 History.com]

As American history goes, the whitewashed history would have all to believe (in that this is all that has been taught in American schools) that the single soul of *Crispus Attucks,* of the Boston tea rebellion, is the only representative of Black presence during the Revolutionary War period. This is far from truth. Moors, who are Africans, were established in the Americas prior to European colonization; as well being amongst the new comers in light of the Moor expulsion from Spain and the Inquisition that was occurring in Europe during this time.

In 1750, "the all powerful deewan of the blacks" proclaimed Sidi Mohammad, the Emperor, as Sultan....He also assisted the Americans fighting for independence and signed the Moroccan treaty of 1787 with the newly formed United States.

The following is a facsimile of a letter preserved in the Moroccan Royal archives in Rabat. In George Washington's own handwriting [and signed by the same], it is addressed to the ninth ruler of Moroccan Alaouite Dynasty (a direct ancestor of the then present King, H.M. Hassan II who is seventeenth in the Alaouite line). The treaty mentioned is of course, the "**Treaty of Peace and Friendship**" signed in 1787 for the duration of 50 years, renegotiated in 1836.

George Washington's Letter to Sultan of Morocco

"Great and Magnanimous Friend" and continued in the following grateful vein;
Since the date of the last letter which the late Congress, by their president, addressed to your

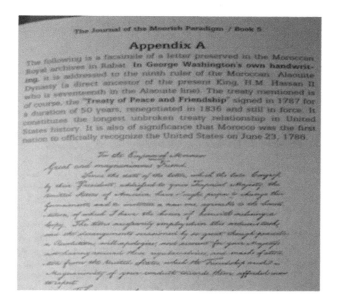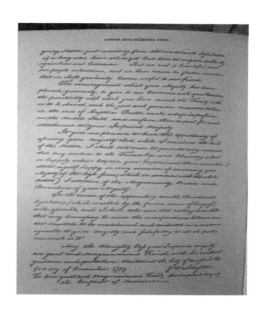

[Ref; Moorish Paradigm Journal, Book 5. Northgate Civilization. 1993-2005. www.mu-atlantis.com]

Imperial Majesty, the United States of America have thought proper to change their government and initiate a new one, agreeable to the Constitution, of which I have the honor of herewith enclosing a copy." [see remainder of translation below]

This change of government referred by George Washington is the *Articles of Association*, which then evolved into The *Articles of Confederation* following the *Revolutionary War*. The first elected president of the *Continental Congress* was *President John Hanson*. Up to this point the Congress and the Constitution was acollaboration between the Moors and the Colonists that met in Philadelphia, the capital of the Moors. A Separate congress then formed in New York. This congress was made up of Colonists only. However, everything drafted in the first Constitution was carried over to the 2ndConstitution and was re-ratified in New York 1789.   This separate congress then appointedGeorge Washington as the new first president. Hopefully you can detect the divisive nature of this second constitution and president.   Every European was of an immigrant status. The Nationality Act of 1790 defined the eligibility for citizens by naturalization and establish standards and procedures by which immigrants became US citizens.

Congress limited this important right to *"free whitepersons."*

[Immigration History.org]

With this, you can get a feel of how from the start of this United States, every decision is and has been made with African Moors in consideration, in contrast to Moors, and ultimately to the detriment of Moors.

The Journal of the Moorish Paradigm / Book 5

Printed Version

"Great and Magnanimous Friend" and continued in the following grateful vein:

Since the date of the letter which the late Congress, by their president, addressed to your Imperial Majesty, the United States of America have thought proper to change their government and to institute a new one, agreeable to the Constitution, of which I have the honor of herewith enclosing a copy. The time necessarily employed in the arduous task, and the derangement occasioned by so great, though peaceable a revolution, will apologize, and account for your Majesty's not having received those regular advices and marks of attention from the United States which the friendship and magnanimity of your conduct toward them afforded reason to expect.

The United States, having unanimously appointed me to the supreme executive authority in this nation, your Majesty's letter of the 17th of August 1788, which by reason of the dissolution of the late government remains unanswered, has been delivered to me. I have also received the letter which your Imperial Majesty has been so kind as to write, in favor of the United States, to the Bashaws of Tunis and Tripoli, and I present to you the sincere acknowledgements and thanks of the United States for this important mark of your friendship for them.

We greatly regret that the hostile disposition of those regencies toward this nation, who have never injured them, is not to be removed, on terms in our power to comply with. Within our territories there are no mines, either of gold or silver, and this young nation, just recovering from the waste and desolation of a long war, have not, as yet, had time to acquire riches by agriculture and commerce. But our soil is bountiful and our people industrious, and we have reason to flatter ourselves that we shall gradually become useful to our friends.

The encouragement which your Majesty has been pleased, generously, to give to our commerce with your dominions, the punctuality with which you have caused the Treaty with us to be observed, and the just and generous measures taken in the case of Captain Proctor, make a deep impression on the United States and confirm their respect for, and attachment to, your Imperial Majesty.

It gives me pleasure to have this opportunity of assuring your Majesty that, while I remain at the head of this nation, I shall not cease to promote every measure that may conduce to the friendship and harmony which so happily subsist between your Empire and them, and shall esteem myself happy in every occasion of convincing your Majesty of the high sense (which in common with the whole Nation) I entertain of the magnanimity, wisdom and benevolence of your Majesty. In the course of the approaching winter, the national legislature, which is called by the former name of Congress, will assemble, and I shall take care that nothing be omitted that may be necessary to cause the correspondence to be maintained and conducted in a manner agreeable to your Majesty and giving satisfaction to all parties concerned in it.

May the Almighty bless your Imperial Highness, our Great and Magnanimous friend with his constant guidance and protection.

George Washington

[Ref; Moorish Paradigm Journal, Book 5. Northgate Civilization. 1993-2005. www.mu-atlantis.com]

Rule of the Moors: From the Halls of Montezuma to the Shores of Tripoli

The Moroccans in Africa are aware of the Moorish connection to America, with regards to Moors being in the New England area when the first Europeans came here. Often not talked about, the Moors had enslaved the Europeans before they enslaved us. Their women were sold [to the Moors] like commodities into their harems and as concubines to wealthy noble Moors. This is the reason why the Moorish nobles were for the most part bleached out, and became known as 'Tawny

Moors.'...The so-called Berbers [white supremacy divisive terminology] is a result of North Africans who also became bleached out as a result of inter-mixture with Europeans over many centuries.

Thomas Jefferson and Benjamin Franklin worked closely with the Moors in the Continental Congress to secure the treaty of 1787. In the Bevan's collection there are over 200 letters to the Bey of Moors from the Continental Congress. There were many Moors in the Continental Congress working with the European Masons (who learned masonry from the Moors), to form a 'Novus Ordo Seclorum.'

[Ref; Moorish Paradigm Journal, Book 1. Northgate Civilization. 1993-2005. *www.mu-atlantis.com*]

[Later and yet], the reason why the Moors in the Southern United States were brain-washed [by Southerner Europeans] out of our Moorish nationality and into believing that we all are the descendants of slaves purchased in Africa was in order to:

1. Get around the Moroccan treaties with America and England which would not allow them to enslave Moors
2. To take [Moor] land in the south
3. Kidnap and enslave free Moors in the slave states under the fugitive slave law acts'
4. To take [Moors] from under the treaties signed by America which said that the "original inhabitants of the land shall be admitted into the union as soon as possible, and in the meantime, they were to be protected in their right to property, persons and way of life.
5. The Louisiana Purchase, Treaty with Spain for Florida, 1819; and the United States Treaty with Mexico.

[Ref; Moorish Paradigm Journal, Book 7. Northgate Civilization. 1993-2005. *www.mu-atlantis.com*]

REALMS

The construct of the world, like the layering of skin, are the many layering of realms that are separated by thin veils. There is a series of electromagnetic grids that are connected through which positive and negative electrons pass as wavelengths of sound, light, and electrical energies. In this way manifestations of organized matter persist in form. This construct makes up the seen and unseen which can be detected and experienced through our senses. These energies can and are often manipulated inmany ways, whereas electromagnetic static is accessible by all yet, used by few who have sought to overstand its functions and uses.

This is the world in which we live; the ebb and flow of life. To overstand life is to overstand its many realms and how they interact. These are the studies that the Ancients explored and engaged. These studies are called *Alchemy.

*Words and concepts defined in the modern day western English dictionary begin at its earliest with Latin which precedes Greek. Greek is the start of European evolution. English language definitions typically focus on the medieval period; this wasthe height of European civilization.

Medieval; having a quality (such as cruelty), extremely outmoded orantiquated,
the period between the fall of Rome and the Renaissance of Europe [600 A.D. – 1500].

[Webster-Merriam Dictionary]

New definitions and words from an eastern perspective are needed to expand our perspective of the African Story (or we must learn how to 'connect the dots') prior to Latin and Greek. There is much work to be done here in western society in order to define the African Ancestral memory and experiences contained within our DNA.

Chem; Kem; means 'Black', the name given to Egypt prior to its Greek renaming in acknowledgement of the melanated Kemetic peoples that populated its cities and thrones; Chem is the root of the word chemistry, the mastering of the elements of Earth, air, water, and fire.

Alchemy; the scientific knowledge of how natural elements work together is the study of 'Alchemy.' It is the coupling of paired energies and their affinities for one another. Alchemy is at the interception of the spiritual and physical realms.

Deciphering ancient works require identifying the specific realm that is being targeted. Study here a sample of variousrealms:

REALMS

Blood (Genetics)	Oceanic	Atomic
Cosmic	Physical (Elemental)	Ancestral
Electromagnetic	Principles& Laws	Spiritual
God (Deities)	Shadow	Underworld
Mind (Consciousness)	Sound (Tones &Words)	Virtual

While many more realms exist, this is a good start. Each realm has its own full body of knowledge that must be learned in order to overstand its complete functioning. As one begins to master each level, they will come to realize that there are realms between the realms. This is what's referred to as 'the unfolding.' You will come to have the ability to 'read between the lines.' Knowledge develops in stages as fruit on a tree; in this way a gradual and orderly enlightenment develops. Without proper order, knowledge in an untrained brain can devolve into chaos. The more knowledge a person acquires, comes the realization of how little we are actually aware of. For this reason, quiet meditation allows one to listen to their inner ancestral voice of guidance. The Creator and Ancestors sit on high and avail themselves to us as our guides to assist in this journey called 'Life.'

Today, only fading remnants of ancestral knowledge remain with us as we become consumed by worldly distractions. Yet, the knowledge of our story continues to swim within the primordial waters of existence. Genetically it remains encoded deep within. It too dwells outward amidst the cosmic rays in the Akashic Records. Knowledge is never lost. [C.I.B.]

The veil that exists between realms is often thought of as a thin film that blurs physical and mental perception. Physical visibility is reserved for the physical realm. In order to see beyond the physical realm, *'Third Eye'* visibility is required. Third eye visibility is the ability to access esoteric (unseen) realms; is divinely acquired; may be granted at birth, whereas it extends from a continuation of previous life experiences; or can be acquired through the study of proper knowledge. Thetransference of experiences between realms occur often.   These transferences occur via *'Portals'* that open and close based upon spiritual conditions. Knowledge of such occurrences is the learnings gained by those who seek it; you must be a *'Seeker of knowledge.'*

When one is well studied, in a heightened state of consciousness, and with correct orientation, awareness increases. The acquiring of ascended knowledge takes time because it takes time for *the Ancestors to reveal, for the* **Akashic Records** *to open:*

The Ancestors work during your dream time. Lay your concerns upon your heart before going to sleep. When you awaken you will have the Ancestors answer.

The Akashic Records are open daily. Download occurs from the cosmic library constantly. It is said, that if we recorded every download, we would be able to fill volumes and volumes of books.

Perform strengthening meditative practices such as*capoeira, dance, yoga, ti-chi, or palates* that teach you how to breathe, control and relax your muscles. Check the intent of your heart; the heart is an electromagnetic recorder. Your organs become your witnesses that give testimony at the end of your life. Treat yourself and others well. You are the *Temple of the Creator* and will be held accountable for how you conduct your life.

I love my Ancestors. I love my Elders. Through the guidance of the Creator, they have maintained an unbroken chain of our *African Ancestral Knowledge* that has yet to reach its highest plateau. We each are a participant in the build of that plateau as we acquire and continue the growth of the knowledge that the Creator has in store. The depths of *Primal 'Watersrun deep'(Aretha Franklin).***Sevan Bomar**is a young scholar and contributor to the continued expansion of the human mind.Unlike the cool discipline of **Dr. Frances Cress Welsing** who limited her writings to realms between the unconscious, conscious, and physical; Sevan soars through many realms in his delivery of a vast variety of literary sources and ancestral knowledge.   To him I dedicate the following chapter, whereas the thoughts in itare primarily recorded from his lectures. My lecture notes of Sevan are too illegible to share with most. As a scholar, I have just enough knowledge to follow his flow and fill in spaces between lines, but I suspect that there are only a few who could keep up. Because the information that Sevan delivers is of much importance, here I have attempted to categorize lectures line by line in hopes that they fall into a more comprehensible order for more seekers to consume.

BOOK OF SEVAN

Blood:

1. The magnetic vehicle is the 'blood.' Records of heredity & diseaseare kept in the blood/bloodline One must be careful who you mate with and know their bloodline inheritances.

2. The Afterlife (past) + This Life (current) = Blend together. Blending with Black people is a [path to] healing genetically forascension. The sign of a God is when you cut them, they will heal. This was the knowledge of Kemet connecting this world to the After Life; Kemet was trying to find a physical way to accomplish a like human. Kemet [too] was trying to find a physical way to accomplish [a way through the After Life], and ultimately to the Great Mother battery via fermentation and embalming to preserve the vehicle inside the physical reality as one passes through the After Life. Once arrived, one must absorb the *prana* from the air. Mummified cats served as the battery of prana. This was a method to escape death, preserve a place for the soul, and to reanimate[resurrect].

3. **Chimeras**; two forces that are primary enemies put into the same body; ex: cat = a reptile + a mammal mix ; lions are mammals with round eyes, a cat is in the lion family, but it has reptile eyes. The Egyptians did this to prove that they can.

4. In the Dogon religion the fire represents the spiritual essence of the *Nummo, and the cows symbolize their biological nature.[The similar story of the stolen fire is told in Greek mythology.] The fifty stolen cows represented the Nummo souls lost to the Earth in the failed experiment to plant a colony here. The symbol as seen on Tehuti's staff in the shape of DNA likely represents the essence of the Nummo. The failed attempt through genetic mixing wasto make themselves as Egyptian, and make the inheritors of Egypt as cows.

[*The Nummo is known through Dogon culture. In their steadfast keeping of their ancient ancestral stories, the Nummo was known as a primal water entity that came to earth when their home planet began to die. In research of the Nummo, there exist many similar stories in Greek literature that, although the names differ, the events are eerily similar. Also, between book references and internet tellings, the internet has given new life to the efforts of Europeans to expand their presence in space and in time where they have never previously existed. The net result of mixing Medieval Greek fiction with Ancient Primal African Egyptian preservations is confusion, a method called 'Arrogance of Ignorance' in absorbing and consuming other cultures; vampirism.]

5. As you go through different phases in your life, your past is still with you, stored in DNA coils. It is kept through your maternal line, recorded on your mitochondria.

[The throne of England is approx. 500 years old, compared to the Solomonic throne of Ethiopia which is 5,000 years old, and is documented in the Bible. The last Solomonic Emperor was H.I.M., Haile Selassie I, born 1892, and served as Emperor from 1930 to 1974.

All dignitaries from around the world, including Churchill, attended the coronation ceremony that included a wealthy entourage and live lions at his side. His Imperial Majesty brought many modern changes to Ethiopia for his people. He also defeated Napoleon of Italy during the colonization of Africa, making Ethiopia the only country in Africa that was never colonized.]

Cosmic Realm:

1. Free visions from the moon have breached the 'holy of holys' as they steal the light from the Sun. They reflect the light of the sun as it bounces off the moon.

2. Our Ancestors exist in the tips of our fingers; being that small gives them the advantage to quirk through the cosmos.

3. Saturn, known as the previous sun, is a place of things that last a long time, [such as] jewels, gems, and knowledge. Saturn is order – Lord of Time.

4. In the moon sleeps the Agreeables & the Disagreeable.the Agreeables awaken when your needs and goals are collective. Non-Agreeables awaken when you have selfish intentions.

5. All celestial bodies are a reflection of what exists in the deep or in the waters. The celestial bodies are the planets or stars – spirits moving in the waters that surround earth, which are pretty much infinite. Their orbits create a pattern of tones, vibrations, or modes of thought. Gods have come to be represented by these symbols.

6. Cosmic bodies are embedded within man and woman. We berth mini supreme beings. The adults must take the ground of the over-soul so that the children can see and follow.

7. **Geomancy**: drawing down the powers of the stars. Symbols are used to draw down energy from the stars so that it can be harnessed. Large patterns of symbols may become the layout of magnetic lay-lines across the planet, or street patterns of a city such as Washington D.C. In the street layout of Washington D.C. the eagle or owl at its center is inverted – drawing down power. Symbolisms are taken from the origins of life.

> Ex: Planktons in the ocean are used as symbols by giving them meanings
> of what man wants you to think of them.

This is the making of false power. When you study self, you are able to unlock [(decipher)] such controls. [Do not be steered as cattle] Release yourself from the indoctrination of the world. Study and know thyself and your purpose.

8. There is no good or bad. There are only energies of positive, negative, neutral, and those in-between. All are within you. You are not just a planet; you are a universe that seeks its harmonic balance.

Planet	Upright Symbol	Inverted Symbol
Saturn	Wisdom	Ignorance
	Fatherhood	Vengeance
	Will Power	Malice
	Patience	Death
Venus	Love	Lust
	Connectivity	Disharmony
	Sweetness	Divorce

Passion	Hate

[Because it is not healthy for man or woman to live at the polar extremes and maintain a sane mind, we must seek the middle ground of balance; not oscillating from one side to the other (yin then yang); a harmonic balance between the two, where neither exists is *nirvana*.]

The Uni – Verse

The Womb	TheMatrix
Sound	Language
Feelings/Thoughts	Words
Electromagnetic	Electricity
Gravity	Imaging
The Mother (matriarchal)	The Son (patriarchal)

Words:

1. Hebrew was originally an alphabet of blocks; unlike Arabic, which is a combo of blocks and curves. When you see Hebrew with curves in it, it is the Yiddish form. Buildings on the 'cubit' are found all around the world.

2. A language is a program from selected stars or angels or angles to bring down the power of those selected stars to form the letters of the language. It is like a music box that presents a lullaby that lures you into a trance. This language plays and replays over and over again. In using this language, you are programmed to believe that this is your story. The language is being played out from the stars, this is why we have *Registrars, Monsters, Masters, disasters*, youngsters, pranksters, ministers, etc. These are characters in the program of a spell. A *Magister* is the coordinator; medieval instructor (magi) behind the scenes creating and managing the language; controls the story (starry).

"Get out of my way! Show me your leader. Show me your God. Show me your rune!"

"Change the code! Lets go down and confuse them – confound their thinking! They know how to build the tower."

This is more like a king in medieval times, not in ancient times, speaking to his angels (angles) or his court [decreeing an order to stupefy the minds].

The tower is 'The Tower of Babel.' Tower = Taurus = Path to Unity.

Letters are changed around and repeated; ABCD is really XBXX. **'X' severs the baby from the umbilical cord or 'the source.' ABC carries you down the path; the English alphabet is the *Gothic language that has been scrambled. Ex: *OS* in Gothic language means bone; the bones or framework of the matrix is the *Operating System*.

The language contains the code that traps people into the matrix that finances wars, governments, and capitalism. This matrix is a modern version of an ancient system of control over human beings [humans as batteries]. The king who builtthis system feels that everyone who enters must be indebted to him. Ex: When we are born into this system, we are born into debt and continue to accrue debt that accumulates and gets passed down as inheritance so that we sink further and further with little escape.

*It is difficult to find a reference for the Gothic Language. (Ref; 'JStor' internet archive.)

**'A' is an ax used to break into the 'B', [the only real character]. Hint: see aleph, the first letter of the Hebrew alphabet (a variation of the letter X).

[The matters of language is the study of 'etymology' which is not an easy subject, and even more difficult when applying it esoterically.]

What is being broken into? The Great Mother, the Goddess, the Holy of Holys. Why? Every time you break into a computer, you do not have to wonder what comes next; the computer will tell you its starry- or story. You just look at the next character in the code.

In the Gothic language there is no 'C ', there is however a 'G'.

Ref;The 'G' too is an X: Giba & GYFU is a 'Gift'; Grimm (Gram): inferred from OHG. Opfertier: OE, UFer – cattle, money, sacrificial victim; Matthew 5:23-24 bupor, gift, sacrificial gift. In the Gothic manuscript (codex Argenteus) Giba is a common Germanic word for gift. (giefu, on, 8yof)

[It sacralizes a battle sacrifice for Odin, where the leader of an army emulates a myth of Odin throwing his spear at the enemy with the formula* "Odin owns you all."]

'A' is a phantom letter; a tool or instrument deployed to access the consciousness or operating system to create a framework inside of the consciousness of 'B' (of authentic origin).

They seek access to the Mother Goddess in order to sacrifice her children to their sun god. Giba – Gifu – Gift; this is why the Masons sport the "G".

This matrix is a modern version of an ancient system of control over human beings. The Gen is a reference to GYN (the ancient language) = the female or feminine force.   That is why the Arabs are hell bent on keeping females covered. They worship the 'Cube', the sun, Aries, Goat, Ram. They don't want anyone to be able to get rid of their debt or get out of the matrix [They seek to keep their monies coming]. The daughter represents the earth and has a womb inside the matrix. Venus = Satan = a feminine power; Gen, the *ori-GIN-al*.

In the bible Baal is the son of Dagan. Dagan was known as the father of all the gods. His name was removed and he became the 'hidden' god. The 'hidden' power is known as the 'Amen'. The hidden force of the Amen exists and surrounds every person n the matrix. However, there are two hidden powers; the Higher power is the Mother (Taurus), and the Lower power (Dagan). The spiritual power of the Taurus, which is your soul, is the most powerful force on the planet. Soul searching is the most important thing you can do. The Taurus field has so many connections because we are connected to the stars. The stars are our language.

13.The matrix language holds you into the matrix. Meditation is the act of silence that connects you back to the Great Mother and self. Language of the matrix is the code that brought you into the matrix. Get rid of the language to get out.

The Creator – 1st Aeon

The Great Mother – 2nd Aeon

Language of the Stars

Elohim& Subordinate gods

Language – words – spellings (spells) of the lower kingdom

Man -- subjects (material animations)

Peace – means to split up. (piece)

Unity – does not mean the 'whole'; it means parts and pieces. (unit)

Kabal – one who is not human at all.

Blessed – blooded; covered by blood.

Live = Evil spelled in reverse.

[The world is made of what works and what doesn't work in equal portions.]

Reverse the magnetic field around you from outward to inward [by methods of]:

Perception	Diet
Care	Knowledge
Love	Exercise
Balance	Meditations

15. The English alphabet has 26 letters – it is missing 26 other letters because there are 52 weeks in a year. (26 + 26 = 52); so there are not enough letters to cover all thoughts, so we operate in a divided manner. The words, tones, and vibrations are scattered. There should be a whole wheel but be have only half a circle that is missing code. The Tower of Babel is about the destruction of the original language. The neck is a womb berthing tones that unlock portals and chambers within our consciousness. The tower must be built back [in order] to ascend.

16. The number of the Kabal is 52 – a wheel. The word A should connect back to Z. It does not [in English].

17. Hence the letter D is half a wheel. Study all of the words of detriment in the dictionary [that begin with] the letter D. Division has many dangers. Because the concept of the Devil was introduced, only a few hundred years ago, to expose everyone to the concept of Socialism – which is Nazism. Nazism is 'National Socialism' – an idea of Superiority which creates division; a mental virus that will continue to play itself out in many forms – whether it divides humans from humans, from creation, or a multiple of other things. This has been engineered and brought to us by the intelligencia to uphold government systems – anything under 'United'; Division – vs – United; Anti-Democracy –vs- Democracy, Republicans –vs- Democrats; all are currently being Hijacked.

18. With the English language we have been cut off by introducing a divisive language.

That is why you see the numerical system hooked up to the alphabet to produce a more logical communication system.

19. The Cusers: the cusers may be seen holding a pine cone. Their goal is to drive a wedge between you and others, e.g. daughter against mother, son against father. Wedges are driven in the center o the back where you cannot reach. Entities attach to the human body on the wedges.

20. When you are able to master yourself then all the other things unlock, because they run on the same code. It takes time to crunch the code, but as you build your knowledge, it becomes your blueprint to break down codes. The blueprint will unfold your ideas that will rapidly become truth.

So then you realize that you have become truth. You [then] cannot speak falsehoods because you are breaking down the words and [now] know what you are saying; you are in the flow [(recognize)] and not one thing you say has been repeated twice because you are deciphering the wheel of knowledge. We are what we think. That is our energizing power.

21. **Whirl = word = world**; tunes and vibrations (mantras). Sounds and thoughts have the ability to penetrate the thin veils or membranes into other dimensions and realms.

22. Words are seeds; words are symbols that when spoken, embeds itself into the mind, and begins to unpack.

23. The rivers are lined up with the constellations in the cosmos. Ancient symbols follow the shape of the constellations in the cosmos. First languages were developed on this pattern. Constellations are symbols within the stars. The Hebrew and Arabic languages follow these star patterns. The correct pronunciation of words gives power.

Inception --------------- to conception

Seed   elements   birth

For those who have taken on the English language in their minds, and have no other variation such as their imagination or ancestral language that can expand their reality of the world beyond the rune symbols of the English letters, the rune becomes embedded in the mind and begins to unpack itself to become encrypted expressions of vast states of thought. The origins of a symbol (rune) comes from the 'over-soul.'

Ex: A 2 dimensional mandala, when unpacked looks like a 3 dimensional
    City, like the pyramids and ancient temples of the world.

A symbol can be personal or put into a collective consciousness in the public space to unpack itself. [This is done in commercial advertisements] If a person is ignorant of their abilities or powers in their use of words, the manifestations may not unfold; or worse, they cause damage. What one thinks about or focus on begins to manifest.

24. There are coded meanings inside of the English language that reinforces itself; reinforcing an oscillation of light, back & forth. We react based upon etymology or definition, which are often incorrect. [Ex: ***Incredible**; in legal terms and otherwise this word means that you give no credit or reliability to the object of this word. Yet, people use it all day, every day. In court, the judge would throw the book at you. Anyone can give an opinion to the definition of a word. Those who learn from listening only and not by study act as parrot that mimics what they hear – from others, television, commercials. Often incorrect practices are promoted in order to confound and confuse the minds of it primary audiences – us.] Yet, it is the vibrational tone (not the spelling nor definition) that is spiritually acted upon; which carry the authentic transformers of power. External phenomena must be confirmed by internal phenomena to be verifiable. Cycle = Psycho; we must break from this circular entrapment.

[*There are many English language entrapments that exist: antonyms, homonyms, anagrams, spellings (spells), dialectics, definitions, contracts, birth certificates, licenses, receipts, and many others. The English language is a deadly science which has been used against Black people for centuries politically, legally, and the entrapments continually evolve.]

Esoteric:

1. In earlier religions the spiritual energies were reversed in both Christianity and Judaism. The moon represented the male – it is now the Sun (Son); The Sun represented the female – it is now the moon; The Jackal of old became Yahweh.

2. **Shed, shade, shadem, shadai**; the shadow realm, as represented by the black *snake (+) and the white snake (-) = +/- = yin/yang.*

Thief #1 (-) and **Thief #2** (-) on the cross with the Christ figure (+) between = energy generation between two polar ends.

Cathonic; dark side; nocturnal; relating to the underworld.

Protestant; a sect that rebelled against the Roman Catholic church during the *Inquisition* of the mid 15th century; as in 'protest.'

Right; rite; a religious ritual

Reich; realm or empire

Fanatic; cult of Baal; possessed with the gods through religious study.

Abraham; father, Ra, Ham = *Ab* is father in the Arabic language, *Ra* is the sun god of Kemet, *Ham* is the biblical designation for the father of Africans.

Solomon; Sol, om, on = Sun of the Creator (energy generation)

Solomon is depicted as interrogating the stars for their knowledge.

Vatican; vacant; the seat of god, but no one is home.

Usurpt ; = serpt = serpent = taken from us

Manual; = man + you + god (el/al); we are the manual; seek within

Baal; Bael = bowel = lower chakra; do not live in the lower realm. Rise to higher realms.

Planet; Plan Net

Story; Starry, from where your soul comes

Prism; Prison; projected matrix

Genesis; Genes; genetic experiment

Division; Dual sight; sion= zion= region; you (physical) separated from your spirit; Causes of division are Love/hate, good/bad, angel/devil. The universe gives back what you have put into it.

Bible; book of babel; Baal; Bael; for the scapegoat. When the Aliens have been doing something so wrong (inhumane) that the only agreement it can come to is a 'sacrifice'; it needs a scapegoat.

Scapegoat; a religious Ram; Scapegoat is to blame someone else by throwing them in the way of what is coming to get them. If we aspire to be like them, then we inherit all that they are running from.

Badges; behind the shield; Hunters

Pray; prey, the hunted

Diet; a way/wish to die

Will; Wheel; controller of your life

[**Mandela Effect**; a method that northern aliens use in an attempt to tarnish sacred African words, by assigning negative connotations to them. This however has been going on for centuries.]

[**Wolf Effect**; in honor of Michelle Wolf and anyone who speaks out against northern alien negative patterns.]

3. Kemetans are the Nagas (Ethiopian for King) Coming Forth By Day – walking out of the Netherworld into the daylight.There are beings and beasts in the Netherworld. The animals are used in an transitory way (womb) to get or keep souls in this physical world.

4. The Anunaki, when they came down entered into anything that had a womb, woman or animal.Letting something into our womb is the same as letting it into our mind or consciousness [as above, so below]. The need is how to [know how to] handle that consciousness.

5. Ra is a name of power – a neuro-network as diagrammed in the Kabalistic diagram of creation.

6. Those who call themselves Israel is not. The G-5 Haploid chains of the Israel pretenders are broken; [as a result] they are a non-caring species. Their god requires cryings and wailings. This is why you see the Jewish priests at the *Wailing Wall*[in the City of David, Jerusalem] rocking back and forth wailing out the Hebraic vibrations and tones. They bring hatred and destruction and separation in their claims of being 'the chosen.' Their god is a jealous god. Their god is Baal.

7. Baal is the god of many faces; the Elohim, Allah, Apollo, Jesus. You cannot escape this god of many faces because it possesses all Kings. The Koran says that the Elohim created man from semen (second creation) as opposed to from the primal waters of the Great Mother (as in the first creation). Luxury is Lux=Light=Life=Nature=Free.The imposter is Baal = Lucifer= the light barer =oil= electricity=debt.

8.**Lord**; lower ladder of light. Those who serve the Lord cannot make it past the lord that they serve. They cannot ascend to the upper realms.

9. The U.S. government structure has devolved into a feudal land system with its well defined Maritime Law in full regalia. The courthouse is a ship docked upon land. They are in league with the sailor. The ship that contains the ark, upper and lower classes, separated through the offspring; dynastic qualities that are codified through the social structure of class – caste system—totem animals that are in direct conflict with other totem animals. Ex: Bird + Snake. Both are reptiles, both are enemies. This codified rivalry has roots in Europe's invasion of Egypt that created divisions of 'Upper Egypt' and 'Lower Egypt'. The codified symbols of the Bird (lower in Memphis) & Snake (upper near Nubia) existed then. U.S. [totem] version is the bipartisan system of the Democrats (elephant) and Republicans (donkey) under one flag of *the eagle*. The caste system encouraged by the U.S. government is by skin complexion in favor of white Europeans and those that they deem as such (East Indians who have a strict cast system of their own implemented by British colonialism) in order to covertly mask U.S. maintenance of their former slave system as referenced in their national anthem. [This involves the covert and overt transference of public dollars to white people in the form of subsidy, voodoo economics, and the recent PPP monies to a tune of 3 Trillion dollars; This, with the continued denial of reparations for slavery (minus one state that sadly offered a very limited 4 million for the entire state).]

10. Mastery is a master over thoughts. When you spread your thoughts are in to many places, you are in all of those places. When you can bring your thoughts to the moment, it is so powerful that they can actually manifest in the moment.

96

11. [Whereas we have lost our names, land, and inheritance] the *'Elect'* will speak for us until we are able to speak for ourselves. Who are the *'Elect'*? They are the Red, White, and Blue. The Blue bloods, the Red necks, the Whites are the mediators between the Blue & Red. [We are on the path of another's; not on our own path. We must re-coop our identity beyond 'Negro', 'Colored', and 'Black' and become sovereign to get out of this system.]

12. Innerstand the tale of **Rahu** and **Katu**; mythologically the snake eating its tail; the *'Ring of Solomon'*; from head to feet, what you think, what you speak, what you feel, what you do; the electromagnetic field around your universe that is keeping the magnetic pole in balance and not opposing one another; a circle has two sides; they correspond to the nodes of the moon (north & south) and controls the rest of the planets – the New moon & the inverted Full moon – 2 sides to everything. You must do the work. You are in charge of your universe. It is the lower world that is responsible for getting us everything we need. The mind says "I want a glass of water" – it is the legs that must do the work to make that happen. The lower world is grounded power. As keeper of your kingdom, it is good to sprinkle gifts to the lower part of your body, e.g. give thanks, honor, lotion, massage, etc.. You are the referee in your kingdom; don't let anyone assail (un-sail) what you have established.

13. How long can you live without air? It is invisible, yet it is of primary importance; you do not need to see it. This is the same for your spiritual powers; bringing spiritual powers into visibility is the equivalent of lighting a napalm bomb. Spiritual powers exist in a place that can handle all of that power. That place is in all of us collectively; so we work from that space and we project into this space. When you do the work, you will find time for the liberty of having fun. Liberty is the freedom of privilege. What is occurring in the externally should not remove you from your higher self. Love yourself for your uniqueness, even before you give your love to others, then you will be able to do the most amazing things for everyone. You are the ancient living and breathing wisdom from the beginning of time.

14. **Cathonic**; dark side, nocturnal.

Western Christians are frightened of the coming of the Anti-Christ because it was to explain what western Christianity is really about. This is the ignorance of following religions. This anti-Christ would bring about the end of the Christ Era. Religion has people convinced that they will benefit from what they are told to do – following the edicts of the church. This is false. [Many have been tortured and put to death by these same edicts.] You can only benefit from what you do. No one can die for you. Because life is eternal and the only thing that survives is truth, you need these life and death experiences in order to progress in eternity toward ascension.

15. The phases of the moon effects all. Western zodiacs mainly go by the code which is the snake that surrounds the universe. Nodes of the moon is the controller of all other systems; Rahu, head of the snake/ Ketu, body of the snake. People are like broken magnets whose node now repel one another. We have been broken by lessons that tell us we are not good. Inside becomes broken and we become our own worst enemy. We then look outside of ourselves and break connections or relations that appear against us, but we are only against ourselves. With this we literally self-

destruct. Our mind creates the disaster that we produce within ourselves. However, you can change [the program] by [the practice of truth and reality, self love, and balance].

16. There is no battle that rages between good and bad, nor one that will ultimately win over one or the other. There is no end, the battle goes on forever. The battle is a filter of souls and we each must pass through it. Good and bad equals portions of balance. Neither has ever won. If one did, we would no longer be here. There is the spiritual battle and the physical battle. When the physical battle wins, you lose to return for reincarnation [to earth]. The soul of the battling soldier will never ascend. He fights a external battle for external forces. When your spiritual battle wins, you win, and ascend to higher realms. When you win, the world wins, as you are an example to others.

17. Animals move based on their instincts in order to determine what their reality is. Man is given the choice of the 'Will' to decide. Although man has the ability to retreat into their animal instincts rather than tuning into intelligence; to accept 'Truth' and learn to master the use of the 4 elements to bring the two forces of the 2 oceans (emotions) together within to gain control (Life Force).

18. Peace exists only within. Love exists only within. You must seek peace within in order for peace to manifest without. You must find love within in order to manifest love without. This going within is meditation, not a prayer. This is no religion. The history of religions has added tremendously to the chaos of the world. The religious leaders are lost. They have not brought good, and they cannot stop the bad. Blessing means blood; in time this wish manifests externally. We each are our own leaders in this search for peace and love.[Don't go around preying on others.] If you wish to bless, bless yourself.

19. When you speak to others, you speak to yourself (what goes around comes around—Law of reciprocity), so chose your words with care; encouragement, respectful, goodness that will support and nurture, and make your life improved.

20. The God and Ancestors are within. The outward man is a disgrace, gives pain, and feels pain. The inward man, which is the soul feels no pain and does not concern itself without. Where can you find nature? Yes, within. Once you have found nature, you can use your mind to create—to manifest. What else can you do with such goodness that one finds within except to give thanks. Within you find the true self and find that you are good. Give thanks. Within you find that you wish good things for self. Give thanks. Within you create good thoughts of love, hope, and security. Give thanks. What can one do of those who prowl about outside of self? Those who live externally and seek to steal, kill, and mame? Nothing. Continue within. Are you creating them out of fear? Do you suddenly wish bad for them? If so, you create fear and ill wishes within that will manifest without. Peace be still.

21. The kundalini goes up to collect the seeds – ideas. Then it comes back down to plant the seeds or ideas into the root chakra to germinate and rise up again. Do not get stuck in the high chakra = madness. Not too high, not too low, live in the middle.

Truth:

1. Many have descended the ladder to the lower realm and have shed their garments and have lost all material wealth, only to find that without all of that stuff, they still Live.The things you have

learned in previous lives, you use in this life. Only truth passes to the next life, and then you learn more. The lies do not pass on; the lies are left behind. In order to pass through the womb, you can only bring the good. That is why you must live in truth. You get the rings, like the rings of Saturn. The rings fortify you and protects you from the winds of seduction and influence, and predators—all of which you do not possess judgment against, because 'all is self.' You must accept your role as the creator of your life. You must accept all. That is when your illumination comes in; your intelligence is all within. If you chose to backbite those who trusted you with their nobility, then you are going to have to 'reap what you sow'. You must now become wise – 'Do unto others' comes into play. The seeds that you sow come back to you.

2.Falsehoods in your conscious state you can recognize; they serve as a great contrast. This is the 'debt' system, and the only way out is to stop judging. You cannot judge – not even inanimate objects-- because everything is you. You are the creator of all that shows up in your life. You don't have enemies because you don't make enemies. No one can stand up against you. You must distill your knowledge of who you are and bring your crystallized consciousness online.

3. Truth divisions: Do you promise to tell the truth, the whole truth, and nothing but the truth? Truth is singular in nature. There are no divisions in truth, so where are we? In the bible after Cain killed Abel, Cain wandered into Nod to find a wife. No one else was yet born in the bible, so where did this wife and Nod come from. Nod is the underworld; Netherland of division. Anywhere outside of Truth is Nod. Outside of Truth, something exists. Once you say Truth, you define it as a division from something. So what is this something? The something is called 'shade', the shadow. Your shadowis not the real you; it is a cast as a shadow of you. It is the realm of Nod, the Netherland. Whenever someone lies, they enter into Nod. We actually interact with these shadows. This is the importance of defining words properly. Words can carry you into Nod. There you become lost. The shadow creates gaps in the light of truth. The process of learning who you are is to wrestle your shadow in Netherland, underground. You have a body of abundance by which you pay with pain. Like a seed, the deeper you go, if you make it back up, the stronger you will be. You must then be strong enough to handle the power of self control. You must first identify the untruth that stands between the real you and your shadow that pretends to be you. You must look within in order to find where you are not centered; ex: too far north, or too much fire. You must find the code in order to make the corrections; the wrongs that negatively affects others; the illusions of the subconscious. The shadows of Netherland actually feel abandoned due to their artificial nature of nothingness that doesn't really belong to anyone. The 'I am' within is the truth, but many are not feeling it because they have been taking info from someone outside of themselves – from the Shade – from "It". You must disconnect from the "It". You must find the words that accurately define what you are actually dealing with; name it. When you rightfully identify the thing in truth, it cannot connect back to your reality. All that remains is the real you; the shadow has been overcome by the light of truth. The end of your journey of looking outward comes with the realization that the power that you seek is already within you; you have the power that you seek.Still (steal) your mind back from the external oscillations of distractions. Exit the land of Nod and return to the light of the sun. [Not everyone that smiles is into the light. Many suffer in silence.]

Knowledge:

1. When you put all knowledge together, then you begin to have a synthesis. The sum total leads to Awareness.

2. The high knowledge was taken by the *PharaohAkhenaten*, then [later] showed up with Albert Pike [a Confederate general, Arkansas statesman, and a Freemason credited with founding the Ku Klux Klan].

3.Those who are frightened by others are afraid of themselves.

4. Those who look back and reflect on themselves get caught up in a loop – a recursion mirror, then you get lost in your own memory. [Time moves forward like a river. Water brings the comfort of hope; keep it angling in a positive direction.]

5. Eastern teachings are concerned with the positive things in life.

Western teachings are all about gloom and doom. [This is reflected in the U.S. goddess who in her right hand holds the book of destruction, and in her left hand the unbalanced scales of life and death as she stands blindfolded.]

6. Why do people look for leaders? Because they have been taught, or indoctrinated in such a way that their center of orientation is outside of themselves. They look outward, when in fact their center of orientation exists inward. Within is how one can connect with the Creator. One must first connect with self, in order to access the Creator. Outwardly, only the mind is engaged. The mind seeks words of inspiration from others in order to move their heart and inner senses. This outward stimuli then seeks outwardly to maintain this external stimulation indefinitely. An inward orientation, however, requires knowledge; knowledge of self physically and spiritually and how these two realms inform each other – work together. In this manner you can begin to ascend in knowledge of self and of the Creator.

7. Knowledge without practice / Practice without knowledge; neither works. You must have knowledge and practice together.

Mind:

1. Seven deadly sins; virus in the mind that cause divisions. We each are a piece of the one.Division is a virus that wastes time and energy; [it is a] negative regulator. The Ancestors always say "Never let anyone steal your joy." Ignorance is looking for something outside of yourself; when you are no longer mad at something, you [then] look for something else to mad at. When you are in control of your world (instead of the other way around), then the external things just fall away; then the higher self allows or guides us to *Awareness*. You must be a seeker. Your journey and meditations build you with benefits to remove the viruses. The system continually throws agitations in front of you just to frustrate you because you have no control over what is put before you. But we must realize that we can only control ourselves. So that is the benefit of training yourself inwardly is to have self control. You create your reality. Stay in wonderland, or get into your higher consciousness. That is why the pineal sits at the center of the brain; so don't get into divisions of

right, left, upper, lower, etc. When you rule from the center – not in dualities or distractions, everything that you create is from you – your kingdom.

2. Wheel = Will = Rule from the center of the Will. Have guards at your ports; eyes, ears, mouth, nose, gut; allow only natural things into your ports for your kingdom. The bodies do not matter and is what causes divisions. It is what is behind the eyes. Look internally. The system makes us fight ourselves externally; this leads to war without and within.

3. Don't get stuck by being angry with everyone and think [that] everyone is the enemy. That leads to nowhere. You must be about the business of building solutions.

4. Many say they have the power, but they do not. You do not want to involve yourself in other's cultures. Where is the Dali Llama now? Where is Dr. York? Stay internal.

5. Psychology is metaphysics redefined to discourage the knowledge of what the *Tantra* physics reveal. It is not just about disorders, but rather an energetic force [of interference]. The [existence of] the spiritual and paranormal is undeniable. Jung & Freud did not want psychologists talking about metaphysics; that would be alchemy. They did not want to include these in modern medicine, so in psychology the five evil avatars are:

> 1. Schizophrenia, 2. Oral, 3. Psychopathic, 4. Masochistic, and 5. Anal

These listed disorders represent the matrix. In order to get the real aspects of the five elements on the compass, you have to flip them 180 degrees. When you unlock the five real elements, you access your power. Like the shades, the five listed avatars above pretends to be the you that society promotes. At birth when you come into this environment, you try to find the tools to navigate. The real tools are hidden from you and someone gives you a manual of rules that are completely incorrect, with words [that have definitions] that do not mean what they really are. You must disassociate from the five variants that act as your shade.

1. Schizophrenia; split personality. The compulsive criticizer. They have mastered the trait of masking. They always wear a mask. These are introverted, isolated, conservative individuals. Intellectualizes everything, even if they are not intellectual, they want to appear intellectual. They are patient, waiting to attack with some critical comment; not to hurt, but just to appear intellectual. This is their way of communicating in order to feel secure.

2. Oral; these are those who have experienced abandonment. They oscillate between abandonment and entitlement; creating thoughts of them needing you. Needy and clingy personality; the belief of needing more than is necessary builds a surplus of everything; consuming more than is needed due to a fear of abandonment. Generally does not take attractive partners, are self-sabotaging in their relationships. Their shadow becomes the retrograde of your objective goals.

3. Psychopathic; all about being in control; being right; domineering; dangerous. A needy person will cling to a psychopath and have a tumultuous relationship.

4. Masochistic; Avoids risks at all cost, lives by 'fear factor', feels unwanted, not belonging. Interferes a lot to try and establish a need of want to be praised and wanted. Can be silent or timid shy demeanor, awaiting validation; or passive aggressive, never approaching things directly; approaches at an angle, indirectly.

5. Anal; materialistic, non-negotiable, need to win. Brings competition to everything. They shun funerals and weddings to avoid emotions and empathy that causes a feeling of being weak. Shut down on emotions, will tear things down to separate themselves as a winner.

You must learn to navigate the psychosis of the mind. You cannot run from everyone. Isolation of self throws you back into of these avatars; you must learn to navigate. Truth is unity so you are supposed to be able to connect with everything, at the very least show empathy. You can help to free people from their avatars by opening your heart, but stay on guard. Recognize who you are not, this gives an opening to who you are.

6. Swiftness is part of the conscious poison. The reptile part of the mind reacts faster than the mammalian part, but it is not stronger.

Physical:

1. Common manifestations within man and woman are:

Organs   Chakras   Symmetry   Mandala   Mantras

We all connect in this way internally and in these things we should be meditating and focusing to get right and grow in knowledge of self instead of giving our energies to outside sources that don't seem to improve our stature, but instead detract [from our stature].

Chakras can be maintained in optimal functioning order through mantras and intonations. It is through this resonance that we have a connection to the over-soul inside of us; it is magnetic. The resonance affects your DNA. The more that you master your own power, the more you control your own destiny.

2. Religion is good for many in that it is a governing of these powers, until a person can realize what is going on. The religion acts as a regulator in this way. There is no god in the sky; one should look inward to connect with self. The energies are within you. Seek ascension.

3. Opposition is our refinement. It is an opportunity to see how we are being exploited. The mistakes that are made are part of the learning process. We think that because we make a mistake, then it is all over, when the truth is that a mistake is a part of the beginning of learning new ways. The work [of learning] has much to teach us. The motivation comes at the end – the anticipated pay check – the outcome! Our goal is unity through inner self workings.

4. There are people in the world that have been born, but not registered into the system; They are sovereign bodies.

5. Trial by elements: The only initiation that you need is to be born. Initiation is happening now by us being in a body. The [true] process is one of mastering the four elements of earth, air, fire, water. This is the process of living. If your life does not require any other initiation, and you take an initiation of any sort, you are in fact removing yourself from the benefits of your inheritance of life – to become in spiritual debt to another.

6. **Amagi** – Sumarian; means freedom; manumission; to restore a person and property to their original status & to erase debts.

Ama = mother; return to the original mother. The world is making you feel like you must pay to live by creating fake debt.

Corporation = corpse; get labor for as cheap as possible, until death. All religious roads lead to Rome; a male cult of inversion and perversion.

The Source= optimal conditions; the farther away one gets from the source, the more hellish the conditions and experiences. Like a light bulb, the dimmer things become; you become unsure, you are less certain what, where, and who you are.

7. In a world of perfection, we cannot realize reality. That is why we must first master the elements.

8. Sovereignty requires protection. This was the study of alchemy; the study of the elements to produce weapons; this is external protection. Internal protection is via spiritual defensive and offensive healings. The higher the realms toward the source, the more refined and clearer things are. The internal begets the external. You must exercise your powers in your life. However, when you are created, another anti-you is created. Don't brag about your expectations. Even your friend's double may not like what you tell your friend and sabotage you. Every sign has a neutralizer: Air neutralizes earth

Earth neutralizes water

Water neutralizes fire

Fire neutralizes air

9. The Great Mother gives love to all her children. This check system provides the fluidity for you to have the keys and control to man your own ship; gives you access to get into every aspect of self; provides the awareness to innerstand what is happening in your kingdom; a whole new adventure of reality like when a boat begins its journey upon the waters.

10. The cycles of rulership always follow in this order: 1. Capitalism, 2. Socialism, 3. Communism

11. When your spiritual battles are won, you win and ascend to higher realms. When you win, the world wins as you are an example to others.

Battles:	to eat	to be loved	fight disease and virus	for identity
	to learn	to be accepted	to work	to meet needs

People find it difficult to resist things that will kill them, e.g. smoking, drugs, fast food, guns, fear, ignorance, unprotected sex. We can choose to live by trial and error, or we can gain knowledge and avoid unnecessary pain and grief. Pain is a payment for being in this world; to learn our lessons and do better in the future.

12. The mind is blind. Your life is your dream. You are an infinite spiritual being, and should live accordingly. Which one is more sustaining, a chicken sandwich, or sun light? One is temporary, the other is forever.

13. When man eats other animals they are eating themselves; like a snake eating its tail. You generate energy that is in conflict. What is occurring in the world today is a mis-innerstanding of esoteric spiritual knowledge being perpetuated by the stagnant energies in the world. When the spinning of the earth is off the wobble and returns to its upright axis, which it will eventually do, we should be returning to a balanced state. The world expands and contracts. The Goal is to develop a

consciousness that withstand these dynamics and to stay consistent.Fire= pain, to learn a lesson. The world is the way that it is because people sign contracts and enter into agreements in ignorance. They focus on arenas where they can control and extract from people through agreements financially, politically, spiritually, etc. Externalized heart senses lead to dislikes, attachments, judgments, and distractions. Theses external senses lead to breaks between the spirit and the mind. There is only one solution and that is to always return to self—You.

14. 'All is self.' All are great, even the ignorant. They are just surrounded by shells. You just need to break through the shells. They too are still great ones or they would not be still walking around. Raise the individual just one octave, then they become unstuck and can continue to generate higher frequencies.

15. Clean water and diet cleanses your bowels so that you can vibrate higher.

16. The melanated man, because he/she is a god, is held to a higher standard.

17. Your 'intentions' is what gets you beyond the external control sphere.

18.

Putrefaction/Petrification	-vs-	Seed
Baal		Nature
Bowels		Feed animals
Deficate/Decay		seeds disperse
Millions of years		germination
Oil / Petrol		trees, nuts
Money		Fruit & veggies
		no money needed

19. Why did the northerner forbid the slave to read? Fear, then fear becomes the devil. They did not want you to know that there is a spiritual side that you have power over. They act as if they are on top , when they are actually on the bottom. They scapegoat someone else by accusing someone else for what it does. So you are no better when you behave as them. Lucifer, the light barer is more blinding than enlightening.

20. If you know you are spiritual, then spiritual laws apply. But if you believe you are physical, then physical laws apply. They cannot take your power unless you give it.

21.[Parental Guidance: If a person can follow the rules of an employer or a prison warden, and cannot follow any parental rules of the home, that person is at a substantial loss in this game of life. It is the children who carry on the name, inheritance, and business of the family. When this is not appropriately carried on, then the estate cannot be formed or continued on the physical plane, and little respect for ancestral guidance is likely acknowledged.]

APPENDIX I

Excerpt from; OUR TWO FIRSTPRESIDENTS

OUR TWO FIRSTPRESIDENTS, JOHN HANSON – GEORGE WASHINGTON
THE GOLD BOOK OF UNITED STATES HISTORY, Full of Gold Nuggets, Price $1
ByJOHN W. CAVANAGH, 243 7th AVENUE, NEW YORK, THE WORLD'S GREATEST
LIVING NOSTRADAMUSIAN AUTHORITY, COPYRIGHTED 1932

INTRODUCTION

REBELLION TO TYRANTS IS OBEDIENCE TO GOD.
(Thos. Jefferson)

With a keen desire to participate in **the BI-CENTENIAL CELEBRATION OF TE BIRTH OF GEORGE WASHINGTON.** In an educational, patriotic and constructive way, I felt that I could do justice to the occasion by completing my book for thinking people upon which I have been working for many years and which contains outstanding, rare and incontestable truths, facts, figures events and characters leading up to the termination of **the AMERICAN REVOLUTION** on October 19th ,1781, at Yorktown, Va., and for eight years thereafter to April 30th, 1789, when Washington was inaugurated President under a proposed **"MORE PERFECT UNION"** and our second Constitution—but absolutely NOT a New Union, for that could never be! Many important and vital facts have been omitted for some reason from our historics, together with the names of great patriots of the time, who aided Washington in his marvelous Victory. It is in my most earnest hope, to be able to place these facts and names, in comprehensive form before the **THINKERS** of or Country and the entire world.

What legal rights had our people to the land called the original thirteen States, until the people, under Gen. George Washington fought the war for the revolution and conquered the British Army at Yorktown, Oct. 19th, 1781, and forced an unconditional surrender to the American people of everything the British King owned in this country, from the Commander of the British Army, Gen. Cornwallis. All the rights of the American people were secured on Oct. 19th, 1781.

One must keep this important date in mind at all times, as a guide first, then next look at March 4th, 1789, the date upon which the present constitution was adopted, and the one under which Washington was chosen President of the United States and inaugurated on April 30th, of that year.

Any person unless dumb and blind, can see a great gap of nearly nine years, of strenuous, exciting and important activity, with an increase of over one million people in our country.

One can very plainly see that Washington was made Commander on the American Army in 1775, before the "Declaration of Independence" was ordered signed by our forefathers on July 4th, 1776, and fifteen long years before the present constitution.

The log, long years between the dates above can be seen very distinctly with suffering, fighting and starvation before we won our independence. What had the constitution to do with the history of these frightful years? Nothing.

"OUR FIRST PRESIDENT" – PROVEN FOR THE FIRST TIME

"THE GREAT SEAL" of the United States of America is the only way to prove conclusively who our first President was and after many years of technical research in history, I am now able to place before unbiased people, the absolute proof.

Other authors of our time have pointed out who the first President of the U.S.S was, but every one of them were unable to prove it to millions of waiting and anxious people seeking the truth on this question. To teach our children deliberate lies in history or in any other way is absolutely criminal and cowardly.

I am the first man in modern times to gather together the documentary evidence, that will be acceptable in any court of equity on earth. Even the courts of China and Japan must accept my proof. There is no appeal from my findings, they are absolutely conclusive and incontestable.

TO PROVE WHO WAS THE FIRST PRESIDENT OF TH U.S.A., it is absolutely necessary to:

First: Go to t Supreme Court of the United States and find the authority of the Presidents, and the "GREAT SEAL" in the year 1803. Thos Jefferson was President at the time.

Second: Find out who the first President was that used the "GREAT SEAL' quoted by the Supreme Court for the first time. The "Seal" is the President's kit of tools; weights 67 lbs., costs $1,250 and consist of the Base, upright, Crown and Dies. They were used for the first time by John Hanson, the first President of the United States of America on September 16th, 1782; there never was any other seal an there never will be any other. Every President was compelled to use the First President's tools and every President down into the ages will be forced to use the same tools. There will absolutely never be any other.

Third: now find the first U.S. Government document ever signed by a President of the U.S.A.— (that is, U.S. Government document number one) with the "GREAT SEAL" affixed to it on the very first occasion that the Seal was ever used. It is U.S. Government Document No. 1.

This document you will find is a COMMISSION, dated September 16, 1782, giving George Washington, Commander of the United States Army, full and absolute authority to exchange the English prisoners of War, taken at Yorktown, October 19th, 1781 and other places, and some sixteen thousand Germans and Hessians besides. Washington had to get authority from his superior, the first President of the U.S.A., John Hanson, before he could make the exchange.

Fourth:--Now, get the resolution passed by the Emergency session of Congress called by Geo. Washington, President on June 27th, 1789, (George Washington was President just two months.)

Fifth: Now find Washington's letter dated July 24th, 1789, three months after he was inaugurated President on April 30th, 1789, asking the Secretary of the old Federal Union, Charles Thompson, for the books, papers and the "Great Seal of the

Federal Union." Washington was unable to sign any official papers of the U.S. Government because the new or second Constitution had not provided him with tools to work with. The framers of the Constitution knew better.

Sixth: Then find in the Congressional records that on July 24th, the emergency session of Congress called by President Washington for the purpose, created the DEPARTMENT OF STATE and also a Secretary of State, (Thos. Jefferson). Then and there Congress accepted the first Presidents tools ("THE GREAT SEAL") of the old U.S. Government, and first Constitution as the "GREAT SEAL" to be used by the first President George Washington, .under the new, but absolutely the second Constitution. The authority of the First President, JOHN HANSON, under the GREAT SEAL, was the one and only authority and has ruled the United States of America and every President down to this very day. Without the least shadow of a doubt, we find now that the First President that used the "GREAT SEAL", for the first time, was John Hanson and we thus prove that he was absolutely the first President of the United States of America, and that George, Washington did not come upon the scene as President until eight *8(years later in 1789).

THIS IS A COPY OF U.S. GOV. DOCUMENT. (No. 1.)
IT IS DATED SEPT. 16th, 1782

It Is a Commission to General Washington for the Exchange of Prisoners of War. It is Signed John Hanson – President of United States. In Congress Assembled.

The very first thing that Congress demanded when the English [British] surrendered at Yorktown was the election of our first President according to the first Constitution, but the country had to wait until the new Congress could meet on November 5th, 1781. The first President so elected was John Hanson, a member of the Congress from Maryland, the catholic State.

He was elected by a unanimous vote of the thirteen states as everyone refused to run against him because of his wonderful work in subduing the rebellion of the twelve states that had withdrawn from the Union, and having the first Constitution of the United States of America adopted: "The Articles of Confederation." The country owed Hanson a tremendous debt for having saved the Union, as Abraham Lincoln did in his day, and they paid their debt with the greatest honor in the gift of the American People, and made him the First President of the United States of America. There were twelve candidates against Geo. Washington for President and he did not receive a majority. There were no candidates against Hanson, as an honor to him.

On Nov.5th, 1781, Congress ordered the Great Seal cut at once for the first president of the United States of America. John Hanson. He was first to use it and every President after him has and must use the one and only Seal made for the U.S.A. and there will never be any other. This is an incontestable fact and only in ignorance of these facts will any one ever question them.

November 5th, 1781, the United States of America, took its place in the family of the great nations, in a lawful and legal manner, and the legality has never once been questioned by any nation on earth. Holland and Sweden were the first nations to sign treaties and offer financial assistance to the new-born nation. This all happened under our first constitution.

Eight years after all this had been accomplished on April 30th, 1789, George Washington was simply inaugurated first President under the second Constitution or more perfect "Union"; but absolutely not a new Union.

The United States of America obtained everything it possesses under our first Constitution, known as "The Articles of Confederation." (See Abraham Lincoln). There was hardly any thing in it that was not transferred bodily over into the second Constitution, although great but questionable efforts were made to keep out a great part. After a long fight lasting nearly three years, they had to submit to the rebellious Southern States in the Constitutional Convention, through absolute bribery, by allowing the south to continue their great racket of trading in slaves. One thousand to five thousand dollars for a human being was a great racket.

(Insert)

First Continental Congress, Phili.	1774
United Colonies & First Constitution	
Articles of Association through King of England	
Second Continental Congress, Phili.	1775
Revolutionary War	1775– 1781(3)
Declaration of Independence	1776
Articles of Confederation	1777 – 1781
John Hanson elected President Phili.	1781
Constitutional Convention Phili.	1787
Second Constitution Ratified, Fed Hall, NY	1789
George Washington appointed President, NY	1789
Nationality Act of 1790	1790
Capital Relocation to Washington D.C.	1800

In speaking of the Constitution one must first know that our people had other constitutions long before the present one was ever dreamed of.

The previous Constitution led up to the one we now know, (sort of an evolutionary process) and which most people think was the first and only one; but as a matter of fact our people had four and for that reason I have attempted to show this in a very simple way, and in language that the ordinary man or woman can understand. It is often said that many judges of our courts cannot understand the "CONSTITUTION."

How can we expect citizens to respect our laws and be good citizens when they can neither read or understand our Constitutions. (Read Abraham Lincoln.)

If you do not like what I write, jump on Lincoln. He was a much bigger man than I. When you wish to fight with any one pick out a big man as you will not get any credit for licking a small fellow.

The FIRST CONSTITUTION, or form of government or laws of our people, was enacted through authority granted by the King of England before there were any states (althoughthey had a UNION) on Thursday, October 20th, 1774, under the title, "THE UNITED COLONIES", and was called the "Articles of Association" (See Abraham Lincoln).

The Second CONSTITUTION was called the DECLACRATON OF INDEPENDENCE ordered signed July 4th, 1776, but signed July 8th. This document embodies practically all of the features of the third and fourth constitutions and is the only one that was never changed and can never be changed. It is the TEN COMMANDMENTS OF OUR NATIONAL GOVERNMENT, and if altered in any way, our nation will crumble into dust.

When the Colonies became States each of them adopted separate Constitutions first, and then the UNITED STATES of AMERICA was created, and took its place among the Nations of the world for the first time.

THE THIRD CONSTITUTION was "THE ARTICLES OF CONFEDERATIONS" and was adopted JULY 8th, 1778, but all the states did not sign, on account of the rebellion until March 1st, 1781.

Article (No. 1) of this constitution reads: "and the style of this Confederation Shall be, THE UNITED STATES OF AMERICA" and proves without any doubt just when the United States took its place among the Nations of the world for the firs time. This a recorded and historical fact (see Abraham Lincoln).

The FOURTH—or present Constitution, was adopted March 4, 1789.

The Declaration of Independence and the Articles of Confederation were not discarded and thrown into a waste basket simply because we were going to try and make "A More Perfect." We did not discard the Articles of Confederation and the Union, because the Union can never be discarded or its name changed under any condition.

You can't take anything away from the Constitution, but you can add to it in the form of an amendment providing it is to give the people more liberty and happiness. Only when an amendment gives the people more liberty and life and happiness is it constitutional.

REFERENCE BIBLIOGRAPHY

Ankeny, Jason. *Biography, Bob Marley*. 2001.

Bingham, Caroline. *First Space Encyclopedia*. D.K. Publishing. New York, N.Y., 2008.

Bo'Keem, Allah Shale; Chaniq, Dierda Baptiste; Kano, Ayala; Ayala, Freedom Allah; Allah, Victorious Honor; *When the World Was Black*; Supreme Design Publishing, Atlanta, GA 2013

Boot , Adrian, Salewicz, Chris. *Songs of Freedom, Bob Marley*. Penguin Books USA Inc., New York, 1995.

Budge, E.A. Wallis. *The Gods of the Egyptians, Studies in Egyptian Mythology*. Dover Publications, Inc., New York, 1969.

Cavanagh, John W. *Our Two First Presidents, John Hanson – GeorgeWashington*, 1932. Library of Congress.

Chaisson & McMillan. *Astronomy Today*, 4thed. Prentice Hall Inc. N. J., 2002.

Cleary,Thomas. *Minding Mind, Translation*. Shambalah Boulder Publishing, 1994.

Coleman, Booker T. *A Survey of Moorish History*. Citrans Atlantic Productions. www.tapvideo.com https://youtu.be/neUTQbHiUm4

Crowley, Alister. *Book of Thoth, Egyptian Tarot*. Weiser Books, Boston, MA/York Beach, ME, 2004.

Fleming, Ferguson Alan Lothian. *The Way To Eternity, Egyptian Myth.* Duncan Baird Publishers. Castle House, 75-76 Wells Street, London, 1997.

Giles, Bridget; Day Trevor; Entwistle, Theodore Roland; Lambert, David; Lye, Keith; Marshall,Oliver; Priest, Christopher. *Encyclopedia of African Peoples*(The Diagram Group) London, 2000.

Hamilton, Edith. *Mythology*. Back Bay Books. New York, N.Y., 1942, 2013 reprint.

Hancock, Braham. Magicians of the Gods. Thomas Dunne Books. New York, N.Y. 2015.

Holland, Julian. *King Fisher History Encyclopedia*. King Fisher Publications, Boston, 2004.

Javed, Tashi. *The Human Anomaly*.2014.

Lane-Poole, Stanley. *Moors In Spain*. Black Classic Press. Baltimore, MD, 1886, 1978 reprint.

Mifflin, Houghton Company. *The American Heritage Dictionary*. College ed.. Boston, 1976, 1982.

Morris, Yao Nyamekye. *The Return*, 2001.

Narmer, Amenuti. *The Secret of the Ankh of Our Ancestors*. Grandmother Africa.com. February 22, 2015.

Ray, Regina G. *Contemplations In Black*. Amazon.2021.

Ray, Regina G. *Balance In Black*, Amazon. 2022.

Roberts, J. M..*Prehistory and the First Civilizations*. Oxford University Press. New York. 1998.

Van Sertima, Ivan. *African Presence in Early Europe.* Transaction Books, New Brunswick (USA) and Oxford (UK), 1985.

Wasserman, James. *The Egyptian Book of the Dead.* Chronical Books, 85 Second Street San Francisco, Ca, 1998.

Welsing, FrancesCress. *The Isis Papers*. C.W. Publishing. Washington, D.C. 1991, 2004 reprint.

Williams, Chancellor.*The Destruction of Black Civilization.* Third World Press. Chicago, Illinois, *1987*.

Made in the USA
Columbia, SC
09 February 2025

52645690R10063